Bite-Size Bible™ HANDBOOK

RON RHODES

HARVEST HOUSE PUBLISHERS
EUGENE, OREGON

BITE-SIZE BIBLE™ HANDBOOK
Copyright © 2012 by Ron Rhodes
Published by Harvest House Publishers
Eugene, Oregon 97402
www.harvesthousepublishers.com

ISBN 978-0-7369-4483-0 (pbk.)
ISBN 978-0-7369-4484-7 (eBook)

Printed in the United States of America

12 13 14 15 16 17 18 / BP-NI / 10 9 8 7 6 5 4 3 2 1

To my beloved Kerri

Acknowledgments

In Proverbs 31:10 we read, "A wife of noble character who can find? She is worth far more than rubies." I am thankful to have married a Proverbs 31 wife. Without her, I could never accomplish all that I do in ministry. Thanks, Kerri!

Psalm 127:3 indicates that children are a gift from the Lord. I am privileged to be doubly gifted with two grown children, David and Kylie. I praise the Lord for both!

Finally, as always, I am thankful to all my friends at Harvest House Publishers. Partnering with you through the years has been a pleasure.

Contents

Fast Facts on Interpreting the Bible

To properly understand God's Word, we must pay attention to a few important rules of interpretation. If we faithfully follow them, they will help us grasp the intended meaning of the biblical writers.

Do not force a meaning into the text. What a passage means was fixed by the author and is not subject to alteration by readers. The authors determined the meaning; we readers discover it.

Pay attention to context. Individual verses do not exist as isolated fragments, but as parts of the whole of Scripture. The exposition of these individual verses, therefore, must present them in right relation to the rest of Scripture. To put it simply, Scripture interprets Scripture.

Make a correct genre judgment. The Bible contains a variety of literary genres, including parables, history, poetry, law, apocalyptic literature, and many others. Each of these genres has unique characteristics that we must recognize in order to interpret the text properly. For example, parables (stories) should not be treated as law, nor should poetry or apocalyptic literature (which has many symbols) be treated as history.

Consult history and culture. To interpret Scripture, we must step out of our twenty-first-century Western mind-set and into a first-century Jewish mind-set. (This handbook will help you do this.)

> Lay hold on the Bible until the Bible lays hold on you.
> WILLIAM H. HOUGHTON (1887–1947)
> FOURTH PRESIDENT OF MOODY BIBLE INSTITUTE

Interpret the Old Testament in light of the New Testament. By approaching the Old Testament through the greater light of the New Testament, we better understand the broad perspective of the Old Testament.

Distinguish between the descriptive and the prescriptive. Is a verse merely describing something that took place in biblical times, or is it prescribing something that Christians should be doing for all time?

Recognize that the Bible uses the language of appearances. Ecclesiastes 1:5, for example, says the sun rises and sets. Though not scientifically correct, such terminology was (and is) an accepted way of describing what the sun appears to be doing from an earthly perspective.

When the plain sense makes good sense, seek no other sense lest you end up in nonsense. Enough said!

Now that we have summarized some important interpretive principles, we're ready to survey each book in the Bible. This little handbook will provide you with the big picture or main message in each Bible book.

The Old Testament

Introduction to the Old Testament

The word *testament* refers to a covenant, or agreement. The Old Testament focuses on the old covenant between God and the Israelites. According to that covenant (the Sinai covenant), the Jews were to be God's people and be obedient to Him, and in return, God would bless them (Exodus 19:3-6). The various books of the Old Testament explain this old covenant and describe its outworking in history. Of course, Old Testament history reveals that Israel repeatedly disobeyed God, violating the covenant.

The Old Testament is the entire Hebrew Bible, but it is only "part 1" of the Christian Bible. Jews question the designation *Old Testament* because of the implication that there must be a New Testament (a notion they reject). To them, the books that constitute the Old Testament comprise the entire Word of God. Christians, however, note that even in Old Testament times, the prophets began to speak of a new covenant that would focus not on external laws but on an inner reality and change in the human heart (Jeremiah 31:31; Ezekiel 36:26). Unlike the old covenant, the new covenant was to make full provision for the forgiveness of sins. This new covenant is the focus of the New Testament (see 1 Corinthians 11:25; 2 Corinthians 3:6; Hebrews 8:13).

The Old Testament is often divided into three parts: the law, the prophets, and the writings. The law includes the Torah, the first five books of the Old Testament, which were written by Moses—Genesis, Exodus, Leviticus, Numbers, and Deuteronomy. The prophets include the four major prophets (Isaiah, Jeremiah, Ezekiel, and Daniel), the twelve minor prophets, and most of the historical books. The writings include the rest of the Old Testament books, including Psalms, Proverbs, Job, and others.

Genesis

Author: Moses. This is confirmed by the rest of the Pentateuch (Exodus 17:14; Numbers 33:1-2; Deuteronomy 31:9), other Old Testament books (Joshua 1:7-8; 1 Kings 2:3; 2 Kings 14:6; Ezra 6:18; Daniel 9:11-13; Malachi 4:4), and the New Testament (Matthew 19:8; Mark 12:26; John 5:46-47; Romans 10:5).

Date: Written between 1445 and 1405 BC.

Book Title: *Genesis* means "beginning." This book contains an account of the beginning of the world, the rest of the universe, and humankind.

Fast Facts

Genesis 1–11 documents the creation and then broadly traces humanity's self-destruction as people turn away from God. In Genesis 12–50, God zeroes in on one family—the line of Abraham, Isaac, and Jacob—through which all the other people of the earth would be blessed.

Summary Outline

1. Creation and the fall of humanity (1–3). God created the entire universe, including the earth and mankind (1:26-27). Though Adam and Eve enjoyed a perfect living environment, they turned from God and catapulted the entire human race into sin (chapter 3).

2. The family of Adam and Eve (4–5). The name *Adam* comes from a Hebrew word meaning "humanity," which is appropriate because he represents humanity (1:26-27; 2:7,22-23). *Eve* means "giver of life" (3:20). Cain, their firstborn (4:1), murdered his righteous brother Abel out of resentment that God accepted Abel's sacrifice but not his (4:1-8). Cain was consequently exiled from Eden (4:9-15). Adam and Eve had many other children (4:25; 5:3-4).

3. Noah and the flood (6–9). God flooded the earth because humankind became filled with violence and corruption (6:1-8). Noah was the only one who honored God (6:9). Noah's ark was about 450 feet long, 75 feet wide, and 45 feet high. In this vessel, a remnant of humanity (Noah and family) and two each of the various animals were preserved from the flood (6:14–9:18).

4. Early nations and the Tower of Babel (10–11). After

the flood, descendants of Noah's son Ham developed a wicked kingdom and began building the tower of Babel. This project was a pagan effort to observe and worship the heavens. God confounded the workers, causing them to speak different languages—thus the name *Babel* (confusion). This confusion caused them to scatter (11:1-9).

5. Abram and Sarah (12–25). God commanded Abram to leave Ur and go to Canaan. With this command, God gave Abram a promise: His descendants would grow into a great nation that would be as numberless as the stars. God changed Abram's name to *Abraham*, meaning "father of a multitude" (17:5). God promised that this nation would bring blessing to all the nations (12:3). But Abraham was 100 years old, and Sarah was 90. How would they bear a son? In unbelief, Sarah offered Abraham her younger servant, Hagar, through whom Ishmael was born. But he was not the child of promise. God's promise was eventually fulfilled when Sarah became pregnant and Isaac was born.

6. Isaac and Rebekah (26:1–27:45). Isaac married Rebekah. God reaffirmed His covenant with Isaac on two occasions (26:3-5,24-25). God reiterated that Isaac's descendants would grow as numberless as the stars, inherit the land of Canaan, and bring blessing to the world.

7. Jacob and Esau (27:46–36:43). Isaac and Rebekah had twin sons—Esau and Jacob. As the firstborn, Esau was entitled to the blessing. When the time came for Isaac (who could hardly see) to give his blessing, he was deceived into conferring the blessing on Jacob instead. Twelve sons were born to Jacob through his wives, Leah and Rachel, and their attendants.

8. **Joseph** (37–50). Joseph, Jacob's favorite son, was hated by his brothers. They sold him to a group of Ishmaelite traders en route to Egypt. Joseph's brothers soaked his robe in goat blood and took it to Jacob, pretending Joseph was dead. While in Egypt, Joseph remained faithful to God and was elevated to a high position in Potiphar's house. But when he resisted the sexual advances of Potiphar's lustful wife, she falsely accused him of assault, and he was imprisoned. Two years later, he was released from prison after accurately interpreting Pharaoh's dream of seven years of prosperity and seven years of famine. Pharaoh elevated Joseph to great authority so he could prepare for the famine.

> *The source of all our troubles is in*
> *not knowing the Scriptures.*
> CHRYSOSTOM (347–407)
> EARLY CHURCH FATHER

Canaan was also affected by the famine. Jacob's sons (except for Benjamin) came to buy food in Egypt. Not recognizing Joseph, they bowed before him. Eventually, Joseph revealed his identity to them, and the family was reconciled (43–44; 45:4-7). Joseph knew God had orchestrated his earlier circumstances to bring him to Egypt (50:20).

A later Pharaoh became fearful of the rapidly multiplying descendants of Jacob and enslaved them. Genesis ends with the chosen nation in bondage in Egypt as slaves.

Exodus

Author: Moses (see Joshua 8:31-35; see also Exodus 17:14; 24:4; 34:27; Mark 12:26).

Date: Written between 1450 and 1410 BC.

Title: From the Greek word *exodus*, meaning "a road out of" or "departure."

Fast Facts

The principal theme is God's deliverance of the Jews from Egypt (Genesis 15:13-14).

The book also documents Israel's birth as a nation, God's giving of the law, and the beginnings of Israel's ritual worship.

Summary Outline

1. **The Jews are enslaved in Egypt (1).** From the time of Joseph's death to the time of the book of Exodus, 300 years had passed. Egypt had forgotten its indebtedness to Joseph. The new Pharaoh was intimidated by Israel's exponential growth, so he introduced a harsh policy designed to alleviate fears of a possible Israelite rebellion. The Pharaoh consigned the Jews to hard labor in building treasure cities (1:1-14).

2. **God calls Moses as a deliverer (2–4).** God heard the cry of His people and raised up Moses to deliver them. In God's providence, Moses had been trained as a prince in Egypt for 40 years. God gave him further training as a shepherd in the desert of Midian (2). Once Moses was

well trained, God commissioned him to return to Egypt to deliver His people (3–4).

3. Moses confronts Pharaoh (5:1–7:13). Moses appeared before Pharaoh and said, "Let my people go." Pharaoh said he did not know the God of the Jews. Pharaoh then added to their burden by commanding that they make bricks without straw (5). God reassured Moses that He would deliver the Jews. Moses communicated this to the Jews, but they were too disheartened to listen (6:1-9). The Lord promised to stretch out His hand against the Egyptians and bend their will (6:10–7:13).

4. Moses brings plagues on Egypt (7:14–13:16). God empowered Moses to inflict ten plagues upon the Egyptians:

Nile turned to blood (7:14-25)	boils (9:8-12)
	hail (9:13-35)
frogs (8:1-15)	locusts (10:1-20)
gnats (8:16-19)	darkness (10:21-29)
flies (8:20-32)	death of the firstborn
diseased livestock (9:1-7)	(11:1–12:36)

To deliver the firstborn among the Jews, God instituted the Passover (13:1-16).

5. The Jews are delivered (13:17–15:21). God led the Israelites into the wilderness near the Red Sea (13:17-22), and the Egyptians pursued (14:1-9). Seeing their danger, the Israelites rebelled against Moses and God (14:10-12). God opened the Red Sea so the Israelites could pass across.

The Egyptians continued their pursuit, but God closed the waters on them and destroyed them (14:13-31). The fickle Israelites thanked God (15:1-21).

6. God preserves the Jews (15:22–18:27). While in the wilderness, God preserved His people from thirst (15:22-27; 17:1-7), from hunger (16), from attack (17:8-16), and from ineffective leadership (18).

7. God gives the law (19–24). God instituted His covenant (19), which necessitated obedience to the Ten Commandments (20) and to laws governing a variety of civil and religious matters (21–23). The covenant was ratified through blood (24:1-8), and the Lord of the covenant revealed His awesome glory (24:9-18).

8. God gives directions for the tabernacle (25–31). God provided revelation on instituting the tabernacle. He provided instructions on materials (25:1-9), the ark and mercy seat (25:10-22), a table for the bread (25:23-30), a golden lampstand (25:31-40), curtains of linen (26:1-14), boards and sockets (26:15-30), inner and outer veils (26:31-37), a bronze altar (27:1-8), a court (27:9-19), oil for the lamp (27:20-21), priestly garments (28), consecration of the priests (29), an incense altar (30:1-10), atonement money (30:11-16), a bronze laver (30:17-21), anointing oil (30:22-33), and incense (30:34-38). God anointed the builders for their work (31:1-11). The Sabbath was instituted as a sign of the covenant (31:12-18).

9. Israel breaks God's law (32–34). After agreeing to obey God's covenant, the people broke it by constructing a golden calf idol (32:1-10). God turned away His wrath only because of Moses' intercession (32:11-35), and the people repented (33:1-11). Moses asked God to reveal His glory, and God allowed His goodness to pass by him (33:12-23). The covenant was then renewed (34).

10. Israel obeys God by constructing the tabernacle (35–40). The people brought offerings (35:1–36:7), and skilled workers constructed these items:

curtains (36:8-19)	golden lampstand (37:17-24)
boards (36:20-34)	
veils (36:35-38)	altar of incense (37:25-29)
ark of the covenant (37:1-9)	altar of burnt offering (38:1-7)
table of showbread (37:10-16)	bronze laver (38:8)
	the courtyard (38:9-20)

An inventory of materials was carefully recorded (38:21-31). Priestly garments were made (39:1-31), Moses inspected everything (39:32-43), the tabernacle was completed (40:1-33), and the Lord indwelt it (40:34-38).

Leviticus

Author: Moses (4:1; 6:1; 8:1; 11:1; 12:1).

Date: Written between 1445 and 1405 BC.

Title: The title means "pertaining to the Levites," who were the priests of Israel.

Fast Facts

Following the Israelites' exodus from Egypt, Israel was called to a new way of life that included a priesthood, tabernacle worship, and sacrifices. This book contains all the regulations for this.

Leviticus also contains ceremonial and ritual rules governing every aspect of life among the ancient Israelites.

Summary Outline

1. Laws concerning offerings and sacrifices (1–7). Includes general laws on the burnt offering (1), grain offering (2), peace (or fellowship) offering (3), sin offering (4:1–5:13), and guilt offering (5:14–6:7). Priests are given special instructions for the burnt offering (6:8-13), grain offering (6:14-23), sin offering (6:24-30), guilt offering (7:1-10), and peace (or fellowship) offering (7:11-38).

2. Laws concerning priests (8–10). Laws are presented on the ordination and consecration of Aaron and his sons as priests (8). They perform priestly service by offering sacrifices (9). Nadab and Abihu are executed for priestly sacrilege (10).

3. Laws concerning ritual cleansing, personal hygiene, and food (11–15). Includes laws on eating unclean animals (11), uncleanness related to childbirth (12), unclean infectious diseases (13), the cleansing of unclean diseases (14), and unclean bodily discharges (15).

4. Laws concerning the Day of Atonement (16). Includes laws on priestly preparations for the Day of

Atonement (16:1-5). It also includes a summary (16:6-10) and details of what transpires on this day (16:11-34).

5. Laws concerning sacrificing (17). Includes laws regulating the location of sacrifices (17:1-9) and the use of blood (17:10-16).

6. Laws concerning moral standards (18–20). God's people are to avoid sexual sin (18). They ought to live in holiness in all things (19) and avoid heinous offenses (20).

7. Laws concerning priestly standards (21:1–22:16). Includes laws on the priesthood (21:1-9) and high priesthood (21:10-15). Certain people in Aaron's line were prohibited from the priesthood (21:16-24). Priests must avoid certain things (22:1-16).

8. Laws concerning offerings (22:17-33). No unworthy animals are to be used in sacrificial offerings (22:17-30). God's holiness must be honored (22:31-33).

9. Laws concerning festivals (23). Includes laws on the Sabbath (23:1-3), Passover (23:4-8), Firstfruits (23:9-14), Pentecost, or the Feast of Weeks (23:15-22), the Feast of Trumpets (23:23-25), the Day of Atonement (23:26-32), and the Feast of Booths, or Tabernacles (23:33-44).

10. Laws concerning tabernacle ministry and blasphemy (24). Includes laws on the daily and weekly ministry in the tabernacle (24:1-9). Provides an account of a man who committed blasphemy and his subsequent execution (24:10-23).

11. Laws concerning the Sabbath year (25:1-7). The land is to be cultivated for six years and then be given a rest on the seventh year.

12. Laws concerning the Year of Jubilee (25:8-55). Every fiftieth year is an extra fallow year for the land, which is to revert to its original owner. This is a time when those who have fallen on bad times have their freedom and property restored.

13. Laws concerning obedience (26). Obedience brings reward. Disobedience brings calamity.

14. Laws concerning vows and tithes (27). Firstborn sons, firstborn animals, and the firstfruits of the land belong to God.

Numbers

Author: Moses (33:2; 36:13).

Date: Written between 1445 and 1405 BC.

Title: The title derives from the two censuses (or "numberings") recorded in the book—one at Mount Sinai (the original Exodus generation) and one on the plains of Moab (the generation that grew up in the wilderness and conquered Canaan) (Numbers 1; 26).

Fast Facts

Numbers documents the 40-year period from the giving of the Law at Sinai up until the conquest of Canaan. It provides instructions regarding how the Israelites generally and the priests and Levites specifically were to handle themselves while en route to Canaan. The book also provides instructions on how they were to make preparations for the conquest of Canaan.

The book forthrightly chronicles the Israelites' successes and failures (occasions of obedience and disobedience) during the journey.

Summary Outline

1. **The Israelites prepare for travel (1:1–10:10).** Numbers begins with a census of the people (1). Instructions are given regarding the positioning of the tribes while camping and marching (2). The placing of the Levites is discussed (3–4). Moses urges sanctification—that is, keeping away from defiled things—(5), taking a Nazirite vow (6), giving offerings (7), the consecration of the Levites (8), observing the Passover (9), and following God (9:15–10:10).

2. **The journey to Kadesh Barnea (10:11–14:45).** The Israelites depart from Sinai (10:11-36). The fearful people (11) as well as Miriam and Aaron (12) succumb to murmuring. The 12 spies give a mixed report after spying out the Promised Land (13–14).

3. **The journey to the plains of Moab (15–21).** This section reviews various laws (15), chronicles Korah's rebellion (16) and a vindication of Aaron and the priesthood (17), and provides instructions about priests and Levites (18) and about cleansing and purification after becoming unclean (19). It also chronicles Miriam's death (20:1), Moses' sin (20:9-13), and Aaron's death (20:22-29). The section closes with a description of the journey to Moab (21).

4. **Balaam blesses Israel (22–24).** Balak hires Balaam

to curse Israel (22). Balaam, however, blesses Israel in seven oracles (23–24).

5. Israel's idolatry (25). Israel succumbs to a rebellious and idolatrous worship of Baal of Peor. This section chronicles the death of the first generation of sojourners.

6. Final preparations for entering Canaan (26–36). Final preparations are made for the second generation of sojourners to enter Canaan. A second census of the new second-generation sojourners is taken (26). Joshua is selected as the successor to Moses (27), and various commands are provided for the second generation of sojourners (28–30). A record is provided of the destruction of the Midianites (31:1-18), the purification of Israel (31:19-24), and the distribution of the spoils (31:25-54). The land is then divided among the Transjordan tribes. A review of the first generation's sojourn is provided, along with words of warning and encouragement for the second generation (33). There was great anticipation of the Promised Land among the second generation (34–36).

Deuteronomy

Author: Moses was the author of all but the last chapter, which records his death (Deuteronomy 1:1,5; 31:9,22,24; 1 Kings 2:3; 8:53; 2 Kings 14:6; 18:12; Matthew 19:7-8; Acts 3:22-23). The last chapter may have been written by Joshua, his successor. Appending an obituary to the final writings of a great man was a common practice in biblical days.

Date: Written about 1410 BC.

Title: *Deuteronomy* literally means "second law giving" and accurately describes its primary contents.

Fast Facts

The book repeats the Ten Commandments and other laws. It also contains a restatement and reaffirmation of the covenant God made with the Israelites at Sinai (Deuteronomy 1–30). The covenant is presented in the form of an ancient Hittite suzerainty treaty between a king and his subjects. Such treaties listed responsibilities, included promised blessing for obedience and judgment for disobedience, involved a solemn oath, and were ritually ratified. God was communicating with Israel in a familiar way.

Summary Outline

1. **Historical setting (1:1-5).** Moses first sets the historical context, noting his location and audience.

2. **Moses' first address: historical review (1:6–4:43).** Moses provides a historical review of the sojourn in the wilderness, focusing heavily on God's mighty acts. He describes the sending out of the spies (1:19-25), the murmuring of the Israelites (1:26-46), the conquest of Transjordan (2:26–3:20), the division of the land (3:12-20), and his being forbidden to cross the Jordan (3:21-29). He exhorts Israel to obey the Lord (4).

3. **Moses' second address: obedience to God's law (4:44–26:19).** Moses describes the stipulations of God's covenant. He reiterates the Ten Commandments (5) and

the command to love the Lord (6), and then he gives instructions about loving each other in the Promised Land (7). He exhorts the people to not forget the Lord (8), issues a warning based on past infidelities (9:1–10:11), and exhorts all to revere the Lord (10:12–11:32). Moses then provides the covenant stipulations on proper worship (12:1–16:17), running the nation (16:18–19:21), warfare (20), interpersonal relationships (21–25), and firstfruits and tithes (26).

4. Moses' third address: renewal of the covenant (27:1–29:1). Moses describes the ratification of the covenant and touches briefly on the law (27:1-8), curses (27:9-26), and more blessings and curses (28).

5. Moses' fourth address: obedience and blessing (29:2–30:20). Moses describes the terms of the covenant and calls for obedience, which would bring blessing. Abandoning God's covenant, by contrast, would bring severe consequences (29). Prosperity comes only in staying close to the Lord (30:1-10). A covenant offer of life or death is offered to the people (30:11-20).

6. New leadership: Joshua (31–34). A leadership charge is given to Joshua, and instructions about the recitation of the Law are set forth (31:1-13). Further instructions on the transfer of leadership to Joshua are provided (31:14-29). Moses' song proclaims the Lord's faithfulness (31:30–32:4), the Lord's care of Israel (32:5-14), Israel's rejection of God (32:15-18), God's rejection of Israel (32:19-30), God's punishment of Israel's enemies (32:31-35), and the Lord's compassion toward Israel (32:36-43). It is followed by an exhortation to obey the Lord

(32:44-47). Final directives are provided regarding Moses' impending death (32:48-52). Moses blesses the tribes (33) and dies, and his leadership passes to Joshua (34).

Joshua

Author: Jewish tradition affirms that Joshua wrote the book. Parts of the book actually identify Joshua as the author (8:32; 24:1-28). Supporting this is the fact that the author was an eyewitness (5:1,6; 18:9; 24:26) who wrote the book close in time to the actual events (6:25; 15:63). An assistant to Joshua—or perhaps Eleazar, the high priest—attached comments about Joshua's death and the events that took place after his death (see 24:29-33).

Date: Written between 1405 and 1385 BC.

Title: The book is named from the exploits of Joshua, who led Israel after Moses died (Numbers 27:12-23). *Joshua* means "Yahweh saves"—appropriate because the book describes how God used Joshua to save His people by conquering Canaan.

Fast Facts

This book focuses on Israel's entrance into Canaan (1–5), victory over their enemies (6–12), and division of the land (13–24)—all under Joshua's effective leadership.

The Canaanites were an evil people, engulfed in such things as religious prostitution, many kinds of sexual perversion, and human sacrifice.

Summary Outline

1. **Israel enters Canaan (1–5).** God commissions Joshua for service (1:1-9). Joshua then gives instructions to the people regarding the conquest of the land (1:10-18). Two spies are sent out to reconnoiter the land, and the prostitute Rahab rescues them from town officials (2). Israel crosses the Jordan (3), and Joshua sets up a stone memorial (4). Joshua renews the ritual of circumcision—a sign of the covenant—for the people of this new generation (5:1-12). The commander of the Lord's armies appears to Joshua (5:13-15).

2. **Israel conquers Canaan (6–12).** This section describes the conquest of central Canaan (Jericho) (6–8), southern Canaan (the Gibeonites and Amorites) (9–10), and northern Canaan (11). A summary of the conquests is then presented (11:16–12:24).

3. **Canaan is divided among the 12 tribes of Israel (13–22).** God gives instructions to Joshua (13:1-7), and the Transjordan is divided (13:8-33). Canaan is divided between the tribes of Judah (14–15), Ephraim (16), and the half-tribe of Manasseh (17). A survey is conducted of the remaining land (18:1-10), and land inheritances are allocated to the tribes of Benjamin (18:11-28), Simeon (19:1-9), Zebulun (19:10-16), Issachar (19:17-23), Asher (19:24-31), Naphtali (19:32-39), and Dan (19:40-48). Instructions were then provided regarding special inheritances (19:49-51), the cities of refuge (20), and the cities of the Levites (21), followed by Joshua's farewell address (22).

4. Instructions on retaining the land of Canaan (23–24). Joshua gives speeches to the rulers (23) and the people (24) about retaining the Promised Land, focusing specifically on the reward of obedience to God and the consequences for disobedience.

5. Final words (24:29-33). The death of Joshua is described.

Judges

Author: The author is unidentified. The Jewish Talmud (Tractate Baba Bathra 14b) says the author was the prophet Samuel, who lived during the time the events in this book took place (see 1 Samuel 10:25).

Date: Written between 1043 and 1000 BC.

Title: The book is titled after the judges of Israel, whom the Lord raised up to assume leadership in Israel following Joshua's death (Judges 2:16). (Joshua had not appointed a man to succeed him as the military leader of the nation.)

Fast Facts

The Hebrew word translated *Judges* (*Shophet*) literally means "Deliverers" or "Saviors." This points to the intended role of these judges in Israel.

Joshua's conquest had been effective, but pockets of resistance continued to plague the Israelites. The judges were military champions who led the tribes of Israel against these enemies and completed the conquest. The 12 tribes of Israel had no other central leadership during this time.

Summary Outline

1. **Israel's disobedience to God (1:1–3:6).** The Israelites had been disobedient to God, for they failed to accomplish a complete conquest of the Canaanites (1). In return, the Lord did not drive out their remaining enemies (2:1-5). When Joshua died, the people fell into gross apostasy, and the Lord subsequently raised up judges to take leadership (2:6-23). The Lord purposefully allowed certain pagan nations to stay on the scene in order to test Israel (3:1-6).

2. **God's deliverance of His people through the judges (3:7–16:31).** The history of the judges and their opponents is traced through seven successive periods:

- Othniel versus the Mesopotamians (3:7-11)
- Ehud and Shamgar versus the Moabites (3:12-31)
- Deborah versus the Canaanites (4–5)
- Gideon versus the Midianites (6:1–8:32)
- Tola and Jair versus Abimelech (8:33–10:5)
- Jephthah, Ibzan, Elon, and Abdon versus the Philistines and the Ammonites (10:6–12:15)
- Samson versus the Philistines (13–16)

3. **Israel's apostasy (17–21).** Tragically, some Danites in the north succumb to idolatry (17–18). Debasement and immorality also break out at Shiloh in the central area (19–21). This represents a sad episode in Israel's history.

*The Scriptures teach us the best way of living,
the noblest way of suffering, and the most
comfortable way of dying.*
JOHN FLAVEL (1627–1691)
ENGLISH CLERGYMAN

Ruth

Author: Jewish tradition suggests the prophet Samuel was the author, but there is no hard proof of this.

Date: Written about 1000 BC, shortly before or during David's reign of Israel (1011–971 BC).

Title: The book is named after the Moabite heroine who is mentioned by name 12 times in the book. Ruth and Esther are the only two books in the Bible named after women.

Fast Facts

Women in Bible times were wholly dependent on men for material support. Therefore, women who lost husbands and sons were in dire straits. This sets the cultural context for the book of Ruth.

Summary Outline

1. **Family tragedies (1:1-5).** Naomi's family moves to Moab, where her husband, Elimelech, dies. Her two sons eventually take Moabite wives, live ten years, and then also die. Naomi and her daughters-in-law are left alone.

2. The pursuit of a new home (1:6-22). Naomi decides to return to Bethlehem, and Ruth makes a heartfelt pledge to accompany her (1:6-18). They arrived in Bethlehem at the beginning of the barley harvest (1:19-22).

3. The pursuit of provisions (2). Ruth and Naomi were very poor. God's law, however, made provisions for the poor. Leviticus 19:9-10 stipulated that the outer perimeters of harvest fields were to be left for the poor to glean. God leads Ruth to glean from Boaz's field. (Elimelech, Naomi's husband, had been Boaz's kinsman.) Boaz shows grace and kindness beyond what the law required (2:9,14-16), providing for Ruth and protecting her.

4. The pursuit of redeeming love (3). A redeeming romance emerges between Boaz and Ruth. Naomi teaches Ruth how to pursue Boaz as her kinsman redeemer (3:1-4). Ruth follows these instructions (3:5-9), and Boaz responds affirmatively and pledges to be her kinsman redeemer (3:10-18). However, there was a kinsman closer to Ruth than Boaz was, so Boaz has to first approach this kinsman to discuss the matter.

5. God's gracious provision (4). The kinsmen engage in their discussion at the city gates, where most legal business was carried on. The other kinsman chooses not to take on the responsibility. Boaz and Ruth marry (4:1-12) and have a son (4:13-17), all because of the marvelous grace of God. Naomi finds solace in her grandson, whose lineage eventually leads to the birth of David (4:18-22) and the Messiah.

1 Samuel

Author: Scholars believe Samuel either wrote or supplied the information for 1 Samuel 1:1–24:22. However, Samuel's death is recorded in 1 Samuel 25:1, so he could not have written that chapter or those that follow (or 2 Samuel). Perhaps it is best to say that 1 and 2 Samuel were written by Samuel and others known only to God.

Date: Written sometime after 931 BC.

Title: Samuel was the prophet God used to establish the kingship in Israel.

Fast Facts

The two books of Samuel chronicle Israel's history from the time of the judges through the reigns of Israel's first two kings, Saul (1052–1011 BC) and David (1011–971 BC).

First and 2 Samuel were originally a single book. The Septuagint—the Greek translation of the Hebrew Old Testament that predates Christ—divided it into two parts.

Summary Outline

1. **Samuel—prophet and judge over Israel (1–7).** Samuel is born to a prayerful Hannah (1), who dedicates him to the Lord (2). Raised by Eli in the tabernacle, Samuel responds to God's call and becomes a prophet (3). The Philistines defeat the Israelites, stealing the ark of the covenant from the tabernacle (4–5). Under Samuel's encouragement and with God's assistance, the Israelites defeat the Philistines and repossess the ark (6–7).

2. The rise and fall of King Saul (8–15). When Samuel grows old, Israel requests a king. Samuel initially resists, but God leads him to anoint Saul, whose popularity has more to do with his physical attraction than spirituality (8–10). Saul leads the Israelites to victory over the Ammonites (11). Samuel meanwhile warns the people and their king against wickedness (12). Soon after, neglecting the law, Saul sinfully assumes the role of a priest (13–14). Further, he and his army disobey God by only partially destroying the Amalekites (15). Samuel thus urges, "To obey is better than sacrifice" (15:22).

3. The transition to David's kingship (16–31). The people look only at Saul's outer appearance, but the Lord looks at the heart (16:7) and chooses David, a shepherd, as the new king. David's victory over Goliath brings him great acclaim (17). Jonathan, Saul's son and the heir to the throne, recognizes that David is God's choice (18). Saul is resentful and pursues David relentlessly to kill him, but David always manages to escape (21–27). Saul sins by seeking to contact the deceased prophet Samuel through the witch of Endor, and God pronounces judgment on him (28). David is victorious in battle (29–30), whereas Saul dies by his own sword (31).

2 Samuel

Author: The author is anonymous but was perhaps an apprentice or close associate trained by Samuel himself. (Samuel's death is recorded in 1 Samuel 25:1.)

Date: Written sometime after 931 BC.

Title: God used Samuel the prophet to establish the kingship in Israel.

Fast Facts

Second Samuel continues the historical record that began in 1 Samuel. It records King David's reign—the highs (his military victories) and lows (his sin with Bathsheba). During this time, Jerusalem becomes the political and religious heart of the nation.

Summary Outline

1. **David's coronation (1:1–5:6).** David is crowned as king (1) over Judah (2:1-7). He tries to include other tribes (2:8–4:12) and eventually succeeds, uniting all Israel (5:1-6).

2. **David consolidates the kingdom (5:7–6:23).** David conquers Jerusalem, moves there from Hebron (5:7-25), and moves the ark there (6).

3. **The Davidic covenant (7).** God promises David that one of his descendants will rule forever (7:1-17), and David responds in thanks and praise (7:18-29). (The covenant finds its ultimate fulfillment in Jesus, who was born from the line of David—Matthew 1:1.)

4. **David's conquests (8–10).** David shows great military prowess in extending the kingdom by capturing some of the surrounding lands (8–10).

5. **David's sin (11).** David succumbs to lust, covets another man's wife (Bathsheba, the wife of Uriah), and commits adultery (11:1-5). His cover-up doesn't work (11:6-13), so he arranges for Uriah to be killed (11:14-27).

6. David's difficulties (12–20). The prophet Nathan confronts David about his sin and punishment (12). David's kingdom is divided, his rebellious son Absalom usurps his throne (14:1–15:12), and David flees (15:13–17:29). Absalom suffers death at the hands of David's armor-bearers (18:1-32). David's grief is overwhelming (18:33–19:8). David is then returned to power (19:9–20:26).

> *The Bible is a letter God has sent to us;*
> *prayer is a letter we send to him.*
> MATTHEW HENRY (1662–1714)
> BIBLE COMMENTATOR

7. David's final years (21–24). David has to deal with a famine, an expression of God's wrath against Saul's rebellious activities (21). The famine ceases after seven of Saul's descendants are executed. The song of David extols the Lord's glorious activities and His excellence (22). David speaks his last words, affirming that the Lord spoke through him (23:1-7). He acknowledges those who faithfully stood with him (23:8-39). The book closes with a chronicle of God's anger against David for taking a census of his military might, a gesture of self-confidence (24).

1 Kings

Author: Jewish tradition held that Jeremiah wrote 1 and 2 Kings. Other traditions say that Ezra or Ezekiel wrote the books. The author was an unnamed prophet who lived in exile with Israel in Babylon.

Date: Written around 550 BC.

Title: *Kings* is the first word in the Hebrew text. First and 2 Kings focus on 40 kings in Israel (the northern kingdom) and Judah (the southern kingdom).

Fast Facts

First and 2 Kings were originally a single book but were divided into two books in the Septuagint (the Greek translation of the Hebrew Old Testament that predates Christ). First Kings graphically illustrates how obedience to God's covenant brings blessing, but disobedience brings strife and judgment.

Summary Outline

1. **A kingdom united: The reign of King Solomon (1–11).** Solomon is anointed and established as king (1). David gives him final instructions and then dies (2), and the Lord grants Solomon's request for wisdom (3). Solomon attains significant wealth (4), builds a magnificent temple in Jerusalem, and urges his people to remain faithful to God (5–8). He brings political stability to the nation, engaging in international diplomacy and making treaties with surrounding nations (9–10). Tragically, Solomon's foreign wives lead him into idolatry. The kingdom becomes corrupted, ripe for division (11).

2. **A kingdom divided: The kings of Israel and Judah (12–22).** Jeroboam and the ten northern tribes revolt due

to heavy taxation (12), setting up idolatrous worship centers at Dan and Bethel. All of the kings of Israel (the northern kingdom) are evil. The kings of Judah (the southern kingdom) are evil as well with two notable exceptions: Asa and Jehoshaphat, both of whom are blessed by God (13–16). Elijah comes on the scene to bring reform (17–19). In response to idolatry, he calls down famine upon the land (17). On Mount Carmel, he challenges the false prophets of Baal (18). Elijah flees for his life from the evil Queen Jezebel (19), but God restores him to further ministry. The book closes with a chronicle of Ahab's and Jezebel's deeds and deaths (20–22).

2 Kings

Author: Jewish tradition held that Jeremiah wrote 1 and 2 Kings. Other traditions say that Ezra or Ezekiel wrote the books. The author was an unnamed prophet who lived in exile with Israel in Babylon.

Date: Written around 550 BC.

Title: *Kings* is the first word in the Hebrew text.

Fast Facts

This continuation of 1 Kings focuses on the kings of Israel (the northern kingdom) and Judah (the southern kingdom). It traces the decline and captivity of both kingdoms. Assyria defeated and deported Israel; Babylon later did the same to Judah.

Summary Outline

1. **Judah and the last years of Israel (1–17).** This section chronicles the latter history of the divided kingdom, providing specifics about the kings who ruled and prophets who performed miracles. Joram's evil reign in Israel provides the setting for Elijah's final acts and translation into heaven and for Elisha's subsequent miraculous ministry (1:1–8:15). Highlights of Elisha's ministry include...

- replenishing the widow's oil (4:1-7)
- reviving the Shunammite's son (4:8-37)
- restoring Naaman the leper (5)
- recovering the axe head (6:1-7)
- thwarting Aram (6:8–8:6)

We read of these kings' reigns:

Kings of Judah	Kings of Israel
Jehoram (8:16-24)	Jehu (9–10)
Ahaziah (8:25-29)	Jehoahaz (13:1-9)
Athaliah (11)	Jehoash (13)
Joash (12)	Jeroboam II (14:23-29)
Amaziah (14:1-22)	Zechariah (15:8-12)
Azariah (15:1-7)	Shallum (15:13-16)
Jotham (15:32-38)	Menahem (15:17-22)
Ahaz (16)	Pekahiah (15:23-26)
	Pekah (15:27-31)
	Hoshea (17:1-6)

Of these, only the Judean kings Joash, Amaziah, Azariah, and Jotham follow the Lord; all of Israel's kings are idolatrous and disobedient. This section ends with Israel's captivity (17:7-41).

2. **The last years of Judah (18–25)**. This section chronicles the reigns of these kings of Judah:

Hezekiah (18–20)
Manasseh (21:1-18)
Amon (21:19-26)
Josiah (22:1–23:30)
Jehoahaz (23:31-35)
Jehoiakim (23:36–24:7)
Jehoiachin (24:8-17)
Zedekiah (24:18–25:7)

Of these, only Hezekiah and Josiah bring helpful reforms. Judah eventually succumbs to Babylonian captivity (25:8-30).

1 Chronicles

Author: First and 2 Chronicles contain no hints of the author's identity. A Jewish tradition says Ezra the priest and scribe (Ezra 7:1-6) wrote the books.

Date: Written between 450 and 425 BC.

Title: The English title is adapted from the title in Jerome's Latin Vulgate: The Chronicles of the Entire Sacred History.

Fast Facts

The books of 1 and 2 Chronicles were originally one book. They were divided around 200 BC in the Septuagint (a Greek translation of the Hebrew Old Testament). These books draw most of their information from the books of Samuel and Kings. The material is presented from the vantage point of Jewish exiles returning from Babylon to Jerusalem. The future looked bleak, but Chronicles gave them hope. The books reminded everyone of God's promises about their land, temple, and priesthood, and they assured the people that God had chosen them.

Summary Outline

1. **Genealogical information (1–9).** A genealogy spans from Adam to Abraham (1:1-27), Abraham to Jacob (1:28-54), Jacob to David (2), and David to the captivity (3). A genealogy of the tribes is then listed:

Judah (4:1-23)	Benjamin (7:6-12)
Simeon (4:24-43)	Naphtali (7:13)
Reuben (5:1-10)	Manasseh (7:14-19)
Gad (5:11-22)	Ephraim (7:20-29)
Manasseh (5:23-26)	Asher (7:30-40)
Levi (6)	Benjamin (8)
Issachar (7:1-5)	

The inhabitants of Jerusalem (9:1-34) and the family of Saul (9:35-44) are also listed.

2. David's anointing as king (10–12). Following Saul's death (10), David is anointed as king (11:1-3), and he captures Jerusalem (11:4-9). A brief history is provided of those who stood with David in his kingdom (11:10–12:40).

3. David's reign (13:1–29:22). Highlights of David's reign include his victory over the Philistines (14), his bringing of the ark to Jerusalem (15), his desire to build God's temple (17), his success as a commander in war (18–20), his preparations for building a temple (22), his organizing of the Levites (23–26), and his organizing of soldiers, stewards, and counselors to serve in the kingdom (27). An aged David speaks his last words to the people and to his son, Solomon (28:1–29:20).

4. Solomon's ascension and David's death (29:21-30). Solomon ascends to the throne, and David dies at a good old age.

═══ 2 Chronicles ═══

Author: First and 2 Chronicles contain no hint of the actual author. A Jewish tradition says Ezra the priest and scribe (Ezra 7:1-6) wrote the books.

Date: Written between 450 and 425 BC.

Title: The English title is adapted from the title in Jerome's Latin Vulgate: The Chronicles of the Entire Sacred History.

Fast Facts

Second Chronicles picks up where 1 Chronicles left off. The book chronicles the reigns of Solomon and all the kings of Judah (the southern kingdom) from Rehoboam through Zedekiah. It therefore covers the kings in the same time period as 1 and 2 Kings, but 2 Chronicles omits the kings of Israel (the northern kingdom). Highlights of the book include Solomon's famous prayer for wisdom in ruling as king (1:7-12), the building of Solomon's magnificent temple (5–7), and the queen of Sheba's visit to Solomon (9:1-12).

Summary Outline

1. **Solomon's reign (1–9).** We read of the wisdom and great prosperity of Solomon in his reign as king (1), his building of a magnificent temple (2:1–5:1), and the dedication of the temple (5:2–7:10). We are reminded that obedience to God brings great prosperity, and disobedience to God brings divine discipline (7:11-22). Solomon has great success in politics (8:1-11), religion (8:12-16), and economics (8:17–9:28). Solomon's death is recorded in 2 Chronicles 9:29-31.

2. **The kings of Judah (10–36).** The latter chapters chronicle the reign of Judah's kings:

Rehoboam (10–12)	Jotham (27)
Abijah (13)	Ahaz (28)
Asa (14–16)	Hezekiah (29–32)
Jehoshaphat (17–20)	Manasseh (33:1-20)
Jehoram (21)	Amon (33:21-25)
Ahaziah (22)	Josiah (34–35)
Athaliah (23)	Jehoahaz (36:1-4)
Joash (24)	Jehoiakim (36:5-8)
Amaziah (25)	Jehoiachin (36:9-10)
Uzziah (26)	Zedekiah (36:11-14)

We then read of Judah's fall (36:15-21) and (70 years later) Cyrus's decree allowing the Jews to return to Jerusalem (36:22-23).

Ezra

Author: Jewish and Christian tradition attributes authorship to Ezra, a priest and scribe (7:21).

Date: Written between 457 and 444 BC.

Title: The book is named after its principal character.

Fast Facts

Ezra records the return of the Jewish people to Jerusalem after 70 years of captivity in Babylon. The Jews actually returned from Babylon in two groups—one led by Zerubbabel (Ezra 1–6), and nearly six decades later, one under Ezra (7–10). The first group of Jews who returned rebuilt the temple (1–2). The second group rebuilt (or reformed) the people's spiritual lives (7–8).

Summary Outline

1. **The return under Zerubbabel (1–6).** King Cyrus of Persia, in the first year of his reign (539 BC), issues a decree permitting the Jews of the Babylonian captivity to return to their homeland (1). Under Zerubbabel's leadership, the Jewish captives leave Babylon for Jerusalem (2). Upon arriving, they build an altar, offer sacrifices, and celebrate the Feast of Tabernacles. They lay the foundation of the temple and establish themselves in the land (3).

Their work in building the temple is hindered by enemies who convinced Cyrus to stop reconstruction of the temple (4). Motivated by the prophets Haggai and Zechariah, the people stand strong against opposition and work on completing the temple.

Cyrus investigates matters, decides in favor of the Jews, and allows the building program to continue (5). His decree for rebuilding the temple is reissued, and the temple is completed in 516 BC.

2. **The return under Ezra (7–10).** King Artaxerxes permits Ezra and close to 2000 Jewish brethren—whose hearts had been touched by God—to return to Jerusalem (7). Upon arriving, they offer sacrifices to God in thanksgiving for God's faithfulness (8). Ezra then engages

in intercessory prayer for the people, confessing their sins (9). Following this confession, a spiritual revival breaks out (10).

Nehemiah

Author: Nehemiah.

Date: Written between 445 and 425 BC.

Title: The book is titled after its principal character.

Fast Facts

The book of Nehemiah focuses on the return of the exiles from Babylon and the repairing and rebuilding of the shattered wall of Jerusalem. Nehemiah also sought to rebuild the spiritual lives of his people in Jerusalem.

Summary Outline

1. **The rebuilding of the walls (1–6).** Nehemiah prays for his people, confesses their sins, and asks God for blessing in exchange for repentance (1). Artaxerxes I permits Nehemiah to visit Jerusalem to assess the city's condition, and Nehemiah reports back that the city walls need to be rebuilt (2). Nehemiah heads up a group of people to do the work (3).

Samaria's king opposes the repairs, but Nehemiah refuses to be slowed. He assigns half the people to rebuild while the others remained on military watch (4). Through Nehemiah's prayers and decisive leadership, the construction work continues (5) and is completed in only 52 days (6).

2. **The restoration of the people (7–13).** Nehemiah discovers a genealogical record that enables the people to be restored to the cities that had been their family inheritance (7). The people then request that Ezra the priest read the Law of Moses to them. The Levites make sure everyone understands the Scriptures.

This initially causes the people to weep, but then they rejoice because they understand God's Word (8). A revival sweeps through the nation (9), and the people make a firm covenant with the Lord to obey His commandments (10). They cast lots to determine who will have the privilege of dwelling in Jerusalem (11), and they hold a ceremony to dedicate the walls of Jerusalem (12). Hearing the Word of God leads to civil, social, and spiritual reforms among the people (13).

Esther

Author: The author is unknown. Suggestions include Mordecai, Ezra, and Nehemiah, but there is no hard evidence for any of them.

Date: Written in about 465 BC.

Title: The book is named after its principal character. This is one of two books in the Bible named after a woman. (Ruth is the other.)

Fast Facts

Esther is distinguished from other Bible books in that God is never mentioned. Yet God is seen providentially working behind the scenes. This book illustrates how God keeps a close eye on His people, and it reveals the origin of the Feast of Purim.

Summary Outline

1. **The Jews in grave danger (1–4).** The Persian king Ahasuerus (Xerxes), after some celebratory drinking, demands that queen Vashti sacrifice her modesty before his court. She refuses, and the enraged king promptly deposes her (1). Mordecai, a gatekeeper for the king, helps his cousin Esther become queen, and Esther finds favor in the eyes of the king (2).

Haman, the evil chief officer of King Ahasuerus, hated the Jews and sought to annihilate them. He accuses the Jews of disregarding the king's laws and secures the king's agreement to destroy them (3). With Mordecai's encouragement and in God's providence, Esther uses her high position to make an appeal on behalf of her people (4).

2. **God's deliverance of the Jews (5–10).** At a banquet arranged by Esther, the king offers to give her anything, up to half his kingdom. She asks only that her people be saved and that the one behind the plot to attack them be judged. Haman is promptly hanged on the same gallows he had constructed to hang Mordecai. (Haman's sons were also executed.) The king then issues a decree prohibiting the killing of the Jews. In God's providence, the

enemies of the Jews are destroyed on the very day the Jews were scheduled to be destroyed. The following two days are set aside as Jewish holidays—the Feast of Purim.

Job

Author: The author is unknown. It is unlikely that Job wrote the book, for it emphasizes his ignorance of the heavenly events behind his earthly suffering. A Jewish tradition ascribes the book to Moses. Other suggestions include Solomon, Elihu, Isaiah, Hezekiah, Jeremiah, and Ezra.

Date: Written probably prior to 1445 BC.

Title: The book is named after its principal character. The name *Job* may derive from a Hebrew word meaning "persecuted one."

Fast Facts

This book deals with an age-old problem: If God is good and just and powerful, why do good people suffer? Job was an upright man who had done nothing wrong, and yet catastrophe overwhelmed him at every side. His friends misdiagnosed the cause of his suffering—Satan was a culprit behind the scenes. Job maintained faith in God through his entire ordeal.

Summary Outline

1. **Job's world collapses (1–2).** Job was wealthy, righteous, and respected—not the kind of person one would

expect to suffer catastrophe. But Satan accuses Job before God's throne, and God permits Satan to inflict suffering upon Job. In rapid succession, Job loses his sons and daughters, his sheep and herds, his servants, and his health. Yet he remains faithful (1:21).

2. Dialogues between Job and his friends (3:1–42:6). Job had initially been patient, but he finally breaks his silence. He wishes he had never been born or that he had succumbed to death immediately after birth. At least that way, he would have been spared all this suffering (3). Job's friends—Eliphaz, Bildad, and Zophar—believe that Job was suffering because he had sinned. Three rounds of dialogue are included in the lengthy debate (4–14, 15–21, and 22–26). In each case, Job responds to his friends' accusations by defending his innocence. Job closes out these three rounds with a lengthy monologue in which he continues to claim innocence (27–31).

Attention then shifts to Elihu, a young person apparently observing the debates (32–37). Elihu suggests that Job's suffering is intended to purify him, not punish him. And perhaps some of the suffering is directed at the self-centeredness into which he has fallen.

The Lord finally speaks to Job and asks him a series of questions that demonstrate Job's finitude and ignorance (38–41). For example, God asks, "Where were you when I laid the earth's foundation? Tell me, if you understand" (38:4). This leaves Job practically speechless. He repents in light of God's inscrutable sovereignty and wisdom.

3. Job is delivered (42:7-17). In the end, God gives Job twice as many worldly goods as he had in the beginning. God also restores the same number of children as he had in the beginning.

Psalms

Author: David was the author of many of the psalms. Other authors include the sons of Korah (42–49, 85, 87), Asaph (50, 73–83), Solomon (72, 127), Moses (90), Heman (88), and Ethan (89).

Date: Written from about 1410 to 450 BC.

Title: The ancient Jews referred to this book as The Book of Praises. The English title is from the Septuagint (the Greek translation of the Old Testament that predates the time of Christ).

Fast Facts

The psalms were collected for use in temple worship. Many were set to the accompaniment of stringed instruments. They include prayers, poetic expressions, liturgies, and hymns, and they express just about every emotion, including happiness, serenity, peace, hatred, vengeance, and bitterness. In the psalms, we find human beings struggling honestly with life and communicating honestly with God without holding anything back.

Because we struggle today with problems and emotions just as the ancients did, the book of Psalms is one of the most relevant and loved books in the entire Bible. The psalms are timeless.

Summary Outline

The book of Psalms seems to be a compilation of five smaller collections (or books). Each of the five collections closes with an ascription of praise.

Book 1 (Psalms 1–41) contains primarily personal psalms relating to David and to the doctrines of man and creation.

Books 2 and 3 (Psalms 42–72; 73–89) are primarily national psalms, some of which relate to the division of the Hebrew nation into the northern and southern kingdoms. A heavy emphasis is placed on Israel's redemption and on worship and the temple.

Books 4 and 5 (Psalms 90–106; 107–150) are primarily worship psalms. They often focus on man's sojourn on the earth, praise, and the Word of God.

The psalms can be categorized by their many themes, including these:

> petition (3, 6, 16, 39, 41, 44)
>
> thanksgiving (30, 65)
>
> praise (41, 72, 89, 106, 150)
>
> penitence (32, 51, 130)
>
> trust in God (4)
>
> Yahweh's enthronement (47)
>
> Jerusalem (48)

the king (2, 110)

teaching (1, 37, 119)

the nation (44, 46, 126)

imprecation (58, 109, 137)

The psalms are a rich genre of biblical literature.

Proverbs

Author: The majority of the proverbs were written by Solomon, the wisest man who ever lived (1 Kings 3; 4:29-34; see also Proverbs 1:1; 10:1; 25:1; Ecclesiastes 12:9). Some of Solomon's proverbs were compiled by King Hezekiah's scribes (see below). Other proverbs were written by unnamed wise men (Proverbs 22:17–24:34). The last two chapters were written by the relatively unknown prophets Agur and Lemuel.

Date: Solomon composed his proverbs between 971 and 931 BC. Between 729 and 686 BC, King Hezekiah's scribes compiled additional proverbs written by Solomon.

Title: The word *proverb* literally means "to be like," or "to be compared with." A proverb, then, communicates truth through comparisons or figures of speech.

Fast Facts

Proverbs is part of the Bible's wisdom literature and contains maxims of moral wisdom. These maxims were intended to help the young in ancient Israel acquire mental skills that promote wise living. In Solomon's thinking, wise living was essentially synonymous with godly living, for one who is godly or righteous in his daily behavior is wise in God's eyes. By contrast, a wicked or unrighteous person is foolish.

Summary Outline

1. **Preface (1:1-7).** The purpose of the book is to provide wisdom, insight, prudence, and discretion to youth (1:1-6). The theme is clear: "The fear of the LORD is the beginning of knowledge" (1:7).

2. **The value of wisdom (1:8–9:18).** Wisdom rebukes sin (1:8-33), richly rewards those who seek it (2–3), keeps one from dangerous paths (4), warns against sensuality (5), motivates the slothful (6:1-19), represses lustful desires (6:20-35), warns against evil women (7), rejoices in God (8), and is in notable contrast to the ways of folly (9).

3. **Solomon's proverbs (10:1–22:16).** Righteous (wise) living is contrasted with wicked (foolish) living in many different ways. People's choices in life bring notable fruits and consequences, so they should choose wisely (10–15). Godly living is therefore encouraged. Toward this end, people are wise to have a submissive attitude to God's sovereign purposes, refrain from strife, seek refuge in God, and respond to poverty by being generous (16:1–22:16).

4. **Sayings of wise men (22:17–24:34).** Wisdom has many rewards, providing things money cannot buy—a good name, humility, and a faithful family. We should incline our ear toward wisdom (22), for wise living is

eminently worthwhile, not only providing fulfillment but also preventing the bad consequences of foolish living (23). Wise living leads to prosperity and pleasantness, but foolish living leads to a downfall (24).

5. Proverbs of Solomon collected by Hezekiah's scribes (25–29). We should seek wisdom in our relationships with rulers (25:1-7), neighbors (25:8-20), enemies (25:21-24), ourselves (25:25–26:2), fools (26:3-12), sluggards (26:13-16), and gossips (26:17-28). We should also seek virtue (27:1-22) and prudence (27:23-27). There are numerous contrasts between the paths of wisdom and folly (28–29).

6. Agur's proverbs (30). Man is ignorant, but God's Word is reliable and full of truth (30:1-6). Agur offers proverbs dealing with evil things that should be avoided (30:11-14), disrespect for parents (30:11), self-righteousness (30:12), pride (30:13), the oppression of the poor (30:14), insatiable desires (30:15-16), punishment for parental disrespect (30:17), amazing things in the world of nature (30:18-19), the adulteress (30:20), the abuse of one's position (30:21-23), wisdom as a key to success (30:24-28), and the majestic qualities of leaders (30:29-31). He closes with an admonition to cease evil (30:32-33).

7. Lemuel's proverbs (31:1-9). Lemuel's proverbs make two primary points: First, strong drink ought to be used as a medicine, not as a beverage. Second, the king ought to champion the rights of the poor and the needy in society.

8. The noble wife (31:10-31). Proverbs closes with a beautiful description of a good and virtuous wife. The wise man knows that inner virtue is far more important than external beauty. A good wife is better than jewels!

Ecclesiastes

Author: Solomon—"The Teacher, son of David, king in Jerusalem" (1:1).

Date: Written about 935 BC.

Title: The title comes from a Hebrew word meaning "one who addresses the assembly," implying "preacher."

Fast Facts

Broadly speaking, this book presents two contrasting ways of looking at humanity's plight in the world. One is the secular, humanistic, materialistic viewpoint that sees life as futile, meaningless, and purposeless (1:14; 2:11,17,26; 4:4,16; 6:9). The other is a godly, spiritual perspective that interprets life and its problems from an awareness of God and accountability to Him (3:1-15; 5:19; 6:1-2; 9:1).

Summary Outline

1. **The futility of human endeavors (1:1-11).** Everything seems to run in cycles. A generation comes and goes and another takes its place. The sun rises and sets. The wind blows here and there. There seems to be no ultimate satisfaction in all this.

2. **The futility of human achievements (1:12–6:9).** Solomon investigates the possibility of finding meaning in

knowledge and wisdom (1:12-18), laughter and pleasure (2:2), wine (2:3), constructing great works (2:4-6), pursuing great wealth (2:7-8), music and women (2:8), worldly recognition (2:9), and worldly pleasures (2:10). He found that all was vanity (2:11). Ultimate satisfaction cannot be found in earthly things (2:17-23). One should thus enjoy life and be content with the providences and blessings of God (2:24–3:13) but also be aware of a future judgment (3:17).

Solomon considers the futility of the various circumstances of life, including oppression (4:1-3), work (4:4-12), being a king (4:13-16), false worship (5:1-7), and building up riches (5:8-17). He concludes there is nothing better than for us to eat and drink and enjoy our work (5:18-20). Seeking mere earthly riches is foolish, for they are fleeting (6:1-9).

3. The limitations of human knowledge and wisdom (6:10–11:6). Everything in the world is inscrutably foreordained by God (6:10-12). Man cannot fathom this inscrutable plan (7:1-15). Life does not seem to add up, and the problem of evil is difficult to figure out, so the best advice is to choose to enjoy life despite life's enigmas and mysteries (8). Death awaits us all (9:11-12), so we should work hard and enjoy life as long as we are on the earth (9:7-10). The path of wisdom provides our best game plan (9:15–11:6).

4. Live joyfully, live responsibly, and fear God (11:7–12:14). We ought to live joyfully, for the darkness of death awaits us all (11:7-8). It is especially important to enjoy life in our youth while still remembering the future judgment

(11:9-10). We ought to fear God and keep His command-ments (12:13-14).

> *The Holy Scriptures tell us what we could never learn*
> *any other way: They tell us what we are, who we are,*
> *how we got here, why we are here, and what we are*
> *required to do while we remain here.*
>
> A.W. TOZER (1897–1963)
> AMERICAN PASTOR

Song of Solomon

Author: Solomon (1:1; 3:7,9,11; 8:11-12).

Date: Written shortly after 971 BC.

Title: Solomon wrote 1005 songs (1 Kings 4:32). The ancient Hebrew rendering of the title of this book as "Song of Songs" (1:1) indicates this is his best of the bunch.

Fast Facts

The Song of Solomon shows the richness of sexual love between husband (lover) and wife (his beloved) (1:8–2:7). God Himself created male and female (Genesis 1–2), and He created them as sexual beings (see Genesis 1:28). Therefore, sex within the boundaries of marriage is God-ordained and is to be enjoyed (see Genesis 2:24; Matthew 19:5; 1 Corinthians 6:16; Ephesians 5:31). In any deep rela-tionship, there is both joy and pain, and the Song of Sol-omon reflects this (5:2–7:9).

Summary Outline

1. **Courtship and falling in love (1:1–3:5).** The young woman—a country girl—had worked for hours in the vineyard under the blazing sun. Yet she was beautiful beyond description (1). She felt likewise about her beloved. She dreamed of him coming to be with her and felt desolate apart from him (3:1-5).

2. **The wedding procession (3:6-11).** One day, her beloved appeared. The wedding procession was grand and splendorous, fit for King Solomon.

3. **The consummation of the marriage (4).** The royal bridegroom gloried in the stunning beauty of the bride. The lovers rejoiced with each other in the sweetness of love as wedding guests dined in the garden. The marriage was consummated as the couple spent the first night together. Joy was abundant.

4. **The struggles of the marital relationship (5–6).** Marital strife surfaced. The wife expressed indifference; the husband withdrew (5:2-8). But affection between the two was renewed, and they were reconciled. Intimacy was restored (5:9–6:13).

5. **The marriage relationship deepens (7:1–8:4).** The bridegroom marveled at the incredible beauty of his bride, and she loved him utterly and completely. They grew deeper in their understanding of marital love, and their relationship matured.

6. **Growing in love (8:5-14).** The couple took a honeymoon trip, and the hometown people looked upon them in amazement. The family reminisced in wonder. The

bride exulted, "Many waters cannot quench love; rivers cannot sweep it away" (8:7).

Isaiah

Author: The prophet Isaiah (1:1 and many other verses).

Date: Written between 740 and 680 BC.

Title: The book is titled after the author, whose name means "the Lord saves."

Fast Facts

Isaiah preached about God's righteousness (Isaiah 5:16; 11:4; 42:6,21; 51:6), warned about judgment for sin (13–23), and proclaimed God's love and forgiveness (54:10; 55:3; 63:9). He prophesied the glory that awaits those who remain faithful to God (2–4; 62–63), and he emphasized God's tremendous power, majesty, glory, and sovereignty (44–45).

Summary Outline

1. Prophecies against Judah (1–12). Isaiah prophesied that God would judge His sinful people through the whipping rod of the Assyrians (1–5). God was repulsed by His people's moral degradation, social injustice, and religious hypocrisy (6). Judah failed to repent, and judgment subsequently fell. But God promised a remnant would survive (7–10). A Messiah would someday bring great blessing to the people (11–12).

2. Prophecies against other nations (13–23). Isaiah prophesied against the surrounding nations:

Babylon (13:1–14:23; 21:1-10)

Cush and Egypt (18–20)

Assyria (14:24-27)

Edom (21:11-12)

Philistia (14:28-32)

Arabia (21:13-17)

Moab (15–16)

Jerusalem (22)

Damascus (and Ephraim) (17)

Tyre (23)

God is holy and will not tolerate sin from any nation.

3. The coming day of the Lord (24–27). The judgment motif intensifies. Israel, her neighbors, and the rest of the world will experience judgment. But God is not just a God of judgment. He is also a God who brings redemption. The one chapter on judgment (24) is followed by three chapters on God's salvation (25–27). Joy awaits God's people on the other side of judgment. Many believe this refers to the future tribulation period followed by Christ's millennial kingdom.

4. Prophecies of judgment and blessings (28–35). Isaiah pronounces woes against five groups: drunkards and scoffers (28), deceivers (29), rebellious people (30), those who make alliances with the enemy (31–32), and treacherous destroyers (33). However, salvation follows judgment. The dry and lifeless desert will become a paradise for God's people in the future (34–35).

5. Crisis in Hezekiah's reign (36–39). Isaiah warns

Hezekiah, the Judean king, of the possibility of an Assyrian attack (36). Hezekiah turns to the Lord, and the Lord completely delivers him and his people from the Assyrians (37). Jerusalem is spared. God then adds 15 years to Hezekiah's life (38). But Isaiah prophesies that the Judean people would one day fall to Babylon (39).

6. Prophecies of Israel's deliverance (40–48). Despite the judgments, God never stopped caring for His people. God will bestow His tender love through the coming Messiah, who will come "to open eyes that are blind, to free captives from prison and to release from the dungeon those who sit in darkness" (42:7). He is "your Redeemer, the Holy One of Israel" (43:14), "the God and Savior of Israel" (45:15). Babylon will one day be utterly destroyed (46–48).

7. Prophecies of the Messiah's mission (49–57). The Messiah's mission will be not only to Israel but also to the entire world (49–50). God's people have been through travail, but better days will come (51–52). Joy is on the horizon for all, but there is a heavy price to pay. The Messiah will give up His life for it: "He was pierced for our transgressions, he was crushed for our iniquities; the punishment that brought us peace was on him, and by his wounds we are healed" (53:5).

God's salvation is offered to people of all nations (54–55). Meanwhile, God's people are urged to be just and righteous (56). A final note of condemnation is sounded for the wicked (57).

8. Prophecies of Israel's future (58–66). A glorious future awaits Israel and all those who seek God. One day there will be a wonderful era of peace and prosperity in which Israel will again be back in her Promised Land (60). The Savior will come (61), and Jerusalem will be restored (62). Israel will finally be converted (63–64), and Gentiles will be saved by calling upon the Lord (65). There will be a new heaven and a new earth. Perfect worship will be restored (66).

Jeremiah

Author: The prophet Jeremiah (1:1).

Date: Written between 627 and 570 BC.

Title: The book is titled after the author, whose name means "Jehovah throws," referring to laying a foundation.

Fast Facts

Jeremiah began his ministry in Judah during the reign of Josiah (640–609 BC) and continued through the reigns of four other kings—Jehoahaz (609), Jehoiakim (609–598), Jehoiachin (598–597), and Zedekiah (597–586). Jeremiah was given a harsh message of judgment to deliver. The people ignored him, continuing to commit idolatry, adultery, injustice, tyranny against the helpless, and dishonesty.

Summary Outline

1. **Jeremiah's call and commission (1).** Jeremiah was called and sanctified as God's spokesman even before he was born. The Lord instructs Jeremiah about his messages to Judah.

2. Prophecies concerning Judah (2–45). Jeremiah communicates his message to the people in various creative sermons, parables, and object lessons. He presents 12 graphic messages that explain why judgment will soon fall on Judah. In gross irony, Jeremiah indicates that pagans are more faithful to their false gods than the Judeans are to the one true God.

Jeremiah attempts to confess the people's sins to God. Because their sin is so great and they are unrepentant, it is to no avail. Jeremiah laments at the sad condition of his people and prophesies that they will go into captivity.

Still, Jeremiah parenthetically prophesies that restoration will ultimately come through the Messiah. Meanwhile, despite the claims of Judah's false prophets that no judgment is coming, Jeremiah promises that they will be in captivity for 70 years. As a result of his dark prophecies regarding Judah, Jeremiah suffers harsh opposition and persecution (26–45). The false prophets call for his death, but Judah's leaders spared him.

Jeremiah repeats his message that Judah will soon suffer divine discipline in Babylon. But he also reminds the people that the Messiah will bring a time of restoration and a new covenant (30–33). A remnant of the people will survive and be greatly blessed.

Opposition continues to escalate against Jeremiah (34–35). Jeremiah is prohibited from entering the temple. His assistant, Baruch, therefore reads his proclamations in the temple on his behalf. The king burns Jeremiah's prophetic scroll and imprisons him. After the city falls in judgment, Jeremiah is taken to Egypt by other Jews. But he warns them that the Babylonians will invade Egypt too.

> *Disregard the study of God, and you sentence your-self to stumble and blunder through life blindfolded.*
>
> J.I. PACKER (BORN 1926)
> AUTHOR AND THEOLOGIAN

3. Prophecies concerning the nations (46–51). Jeremiah then issues prophetic proclamations against other nations:

Egypt (46:2-28)	Damascus (49:23-27)
Philistia (47)	Kedar and Hazor (49:28-33)
Moab (48)	Elam (49:34-39)
Ammon (49:1-6)	Babylon (50–51)
Edom (49:7-22)	

No sinful and unrepentant nation escapes judgment.

4. The fall of Jerusalem (52). Finally, as warned, Jerusalem falls. The city is destroyed (52:1-23), the leaders killed, and the Jewish common-folk deported to Babylon (52:24-30).

Lamentations

Author: The prophet Jeremiah (see 2 Chronicles 35:25).
Date: Written in about 586 BC.

Title: The title comes from the title in the Latin version, which means "loud cries."

Fast Facts

Jeremiah seems to have witnessed the destruction of Jerusalem firsthand (1:13-15; 2:6,9; 4:1-12). The people were deported to live in Babylon in exile. This is the only book in the Bible that consists solely of laments and contains five melancholy poems of mourning over the Babylonians' complete destruction of Jerusalem and its temple.

Summary Outline

1. **The first lament: the desolation of Jerusalem (1).** Jeremiah mourns the destruction of Jerusalem. For more than 40 years, he had been warning it would come, but the people never listened. When the Babylonians finally overthrow the city, Jeremiah compassionately identifies with his people and laments with them.

2. **The second lament: God's punishment of Jerusalem (2).** The Babylonians destroyed the city, but Babylon was merely the whipping cord of the Lord.

3. **The third lament: Jeremiah's grief (3).** Jeremiah expresses grief over this state of affairs. He prays for God's mercy and the restoration of his people.

4. **The fourth lament: The Lord's anger (4).** Jeremiah reflects on how severely the city of Jerusalem had been judged by the Lord in His anger. He considers that the sins of the people, prophets, and priests brought all this about.

5. **The fifth lament: The remnant's response (5).** The

Jews in captivity reflect on their horrific state of affairs. They yearn and pray for deliverance and restoration.

Ezekiel

Author: The prophet Ezekiel, the son of Buzi (1:3).

Date: Written between 593 and 570 BC.

Title: The book is named after the author.

Fast Facts

Ezekiel communicated in a unique way, dramatizing God's message by using signs, symbols, and parables. During the first part of his ministry, he graphically communicated that God's judgment falls as a result of human sin. After Babylon took the Jews into exile, Ezekiel spoke words of hope and comfort.

Summary Outline

1. **Ezekiel's call and commission (1–3).** God calls and commissions Ezekiel as His mouthpiece to Judah. Ezekiel witnesses God's glory in an incredible vision that will stick with him through his entire ministry. God then gives him instructions and empowers him for his task.

2. **God's judgment on Judah (4–24).** Ezekiel prophesies a coming judgment on Judah. This judgment is an absolute certainty (4–7). Ezekiel speaks of Judah's sins and abominations and the subsequent departure of God's glory from the temple. Both the common people and the

religious leaders are guilty (8–11). Judah is brimming with false prophets who lead the people astray and give them a false sense of security. Ezekiel uses graphic metaphors to illustrate the dire condition of the people. They are like a vine without fruit or a wife who had committed adultery. God will therefore use the Babylonians as His whipping cord to judge Judah. Yet Ezekiel also indicates that God will restore His people in the future (12–24).

3. God's judgment on the Gentile nations (25–32). Judah's judgment and downfall are not a cause for celebration among the surrounding nations. They too are ripe for judgment, and it will surely fall on…

Ammon (25:1-7)	Tyre (26:1–28:19)
Moab (25:8-11)	Sidon (28:20-24)
Edom (25:12-14)	and Egypt (29–32)
Philistia (25:15-17)	

4. God's blessings on Israel (33–48). God has a future for His people. In this final section, Ezekiel no longer speaks about judgment, but rather focuses on the comfort and consolation of God's people in view of a glorious future (33–35).

God's people will one day be regathered and restored. Ezekiel has a vision of the bones of a skeleton coming back together, muscles growing on the bones, skin covering the muscles, and God breathing life into them. This graphic metaphor indicates that God will one day gather His people and animate the nation by the Spirit of God (36–37).

Ezekiel also speaks of a future invasion of a northern military coalition into Israel. But God Himself will rescue His people from this invasion (38–39).

Finally, Ezekiel describes a millennial temple to which the glory of the Lord will return (40–48). God indeed has a future plan for His people!

Daniel

Author: The prophet Daniel (see 8:15,27; 9:2; 10:2,7; 12:4-5).

Date: Written in approximately 537 BC.

Title: The book is named after the author.

Fast Facts

The book of Daniel contains apocalyptic prophecies of the end times. Daniel speaks of a revived Roman Empire over which the Antichrist will rule (2; 7). Daniel's most famous prophesy is of 70 sevens (or weeks). The seventieth week (Daniel 9:26-27) is the tribulation period that immediately precedes the second coming of Christ.

Summary Outline

1. **Daniel's personal history (1).** Daniel is deported to Babylon, where he and other young men are trained to serve in Nebuchadnezzar's court. Their names and diets are changed. Daniel, however, remains faithful to the Lord, refusing to eat food dedicated to idols, and the Lord rewards him for this.

2. God's prophetic plan for the Gentiles (2–7). Daniel is able to interpret Nebuchadnezzar's disturbing dream of a great statue (2). God will raise up and then bring down four Gentile empires—the fourth being a revived Roman Empire over which the Antichrist will rule. The times of the Gentiles will finally end at the second coming of Jesus Christ.

Nebuchadnezzar sets up a golden image and decrees that all bow to it (3:1-7). Daniel and his friends refuse and are subsequently tossed into a furnace as punishment. But God delivers them, and they are all promoted (3:8-30).

The self-inflated, prideful Nebuchadnezzar then has a dream indicating that God will bring him down and humiliate him for a time, causing him to dwell with animals. Nebuchadnezzar is eventually restored and afterward offers praises to God (4).

Belshazzar, Babylon's next king, arrogantly defies God. He sees handwriting on the wall: "Your kingdom is numbered, weighed, and divided." That very night, the kingdom of the Babylonians falls to Darius and the Medes (5).

Darius decrees that no one can pray to any god other than Darius himself. Daniel refuses and is thrown into a den of lions overnight. But God delivers Daniel, and Daniel is exalted even higher (6).

Daniel then has a vision of four strange beasts that represent four important kingdoms in biblical prophecy: Babylon, Medo-Persia, Greece, and a revived Roman Empire (7). (The Antichrist will rule over this future empire during the tribulation.)

3. God's prophetic plan for Israel (8–12). God yet has a plan for Israel. Daniel speaks of 70 weeks of years, which provide a prophetic timetable for Israel (9). Israel's timetable is divided into 70 groups of 7 years, totaling 490 years. The first 69 groups of 7 years—or 483 years—began with the issuing of a decree to restore and rebuild Jerusalem and ended with the coming of Jesus the Messiah (9:25). After that, God's prophetic clock stopped. Daniel predicted the gap between these 483 years and the final 7 years of Israel's prophetic timetable.

> *There are four things that we ought to do*
> *with the Word of God—admit it as the Word of God,*
> *commit it to our hearts and minds,*
> *submit to it, and transmit it to the world.*
> WILLIAM WILBERFORCE (1759–1833)
> ANTISLAVERY ACTIVIST

The final seven years will begin for Israel when the Antichrist confirms a covenant for 7 years (9:27). When this peace pact is signed, the tribulation period will begin.

Daniel becomes frightened at this momentous vision. He prays to the Lord for strength, and an angel eventually arrives in answer to the prayer. The angel promises to show Daniel further things to come in the prophetic future (10).

Daniel reveals that the Antichrist will emerge in the end times and will "set out in a great rage to destroy and annihilate many" (11:44). The tribulation period "will be a time of distress such as has not happened from the beginning of nations until then" (12:1). Daniel is instructed to "roll up and seal the words of the scroll until the time of the end. Many will go here and there to increase knowledge" (12:4). Many believe we are now living in the days of which Daniel spoke.

Hosea

Author: The prophet Hosea, the son of Beeri (1:1).

Date: Written about 710 BC.

Title: The book is named after the author.

Fast Facts

This touching book depicts the heartfelt pain Hosea suffered at the unfaithfulness of his wife. This gave the prophet a deep insight to the way God feels when His own people are unfaithful to Him. Just as Gomer had been unfaithful to the marriage covenant, so the Israelites had been unfaithful to the covenant God made with them (2:2-5; 6:4-11; 8:1-14). They committed spiritual adultery and turned away from God just as Gomer had committed physical adultery. In their unfaithfulness, the Israelites engaged in adulterous relationships with Canaanite deities (such as Baal).

Summary Outline

1. **An adulterous wife loved by a faithful husband (1–3).** Hosea marries a woman named Gomer. They have three children together, each named by God to communicate something about God's coming judgment upon Israel. *Jezreel* means "God scatters," *Lo-Ruhamah* means "Not pitied,"

and *Lo-Ammi* means "Not my people." God will scatter His people, showing no pity, because of the way they have acted. Just as Gomer ran after other men, so Israel ran after other gods. Yet Hosea continues to love Gomer. Despite her unfaithfulness, Hosea redeems her from a slave market and restores her.

2. An adulterous Israel loved by a faithful God (4–14). Because Gomer broke Hosea's heart, Hosea could understand the heartbreak God felt over His wayward people. The unrelenting love Hosea shows Gomer illustrates God's covenant love for His people. Yet despite God's constant appeal to the people to repent, they refuse to turn back to Him, and their hearts progressively harden. They continue to disobey God's commandments, showing no sign of remorse and no indication of forthcoming repentance. God desires to heal and restore His people, but they continue in their rebellion against Him (4–9).

As a result, God has no choice but to judge them. The fruit of their disobedience was dispersion (10). They refuse repentance, so God has to refuse further mercy. Like the other Old Testament prophets, however, Hosea emphasizes that God, in His faithful covenant love, will ultimately restore and bless His wayward people. He will finally turn away His anger and shower love upon them (11–14).

Joel

Author: The prophet Joel, son of Pethuel (1:1).
Date: Written in about 835 BC.

Title: The book is named after the author.

Fast Facts

A catastrophic swarm of locusts assaulted the land of Judah, eating up the agricultural produce and darkening the sun. Joel saw in this catastrophe a foretaste of the day of judgment that was surely coming upon God's people (1:15–2:11).

Summary Outline

1. **The locust plague (1).** Joel describes the day of the Lord as it was currently manifested—a devastating swarm of locusts had annihilated the land of Judah, resulting in widespread famine and drought (1:2-12). There was a subsequent call to repentance (1:13-20).

2. **The coming day of the Lord (2:1-11).** Joel now switches his perspective to the end-times day of the Lord. The locust invasion is a graphic metaphor pointing to the more intensive visitation from the Lord in the end times. The locust invasion will seem mild compared to the judgments during the eschatological day of the Lord.

3. **A call to repentance (2:12-17).** Joel calls the people to turn from their evil ways and commit themselves to the Lord. If the people listen and repent, they will avert disaster. Unfortunately, the people do not listen.

4. **Forgiveness and restoration (2:18-32).** Despite the fact that harsh eschatological judgment is coming, God promises His people that their time of suffering will be followed by both material (2:18-27) and spiritual (2:28-32) blessing. God will not forget His people.

5. Israel's glorious future (3). Joel prophesies about an eschatological judgment of the nations in which they will have to give account to God for their rebellion against Him (3:1-16). Nevertheless, God will finally dwell with His people (3:17-21).

Amos

Author: The prophet Amos (1:1), a shepherd.

Date: Written about 755 BC.

Title: The book is named after the author, whose name means "burden bearer."

Fast Facts

Amos focuses on the social injustices of his day. During this time of relative prosperity, the rich did nothing to aid the disadvantaged. Ironically, the rich people of Amos' day thought they were blessed with such great wealth because they were so religious. Amos prophesied that a day of judgment and destruction was coming.

Summary Outline

1. Judgments against the nations (1–2). Amos pronounces judgment against Syria for its brutal cruelty (1:3-5), Philistia for engaging in slavery (1:6-8), Phoenicia for breaking a treaty (1:9-10), Edom for its vengeful nature (1:11-12), Ammon for its violent nature (1:13-15), Moab for its unjust practices (2:1-3), and Judah for not honoring the law (2:4-6). Amos then targets Israel for not honoring the law (2:6-16).

2. Judgments against Israel (3–6). Amos gives three sermons, each beginning with the phrase "Hear this word." The first pronounces judgment against Israel because of its iniquities (3). The second delineates Israel's crimes and God's discipline (4). The third specifies Israel's sins and calls the people to repentance (5–6). They refuse and will therefore experience the judgment of exile.

3. Visions of judgment and restoration (7–9). Amos records five visions pointing to God's judgment. His vision of locusts is an apt metaphor for God's wrath (7:1-3). His vision of fire points to the drought that will follow the locust plague (7:4-6). His vision of the plum line reveals that God has measured Israel by the rule of His justice and found the nation falling short (7:7-9). His vision of a basket of summer fruit indicates that the people's fruitful years of prosperity have now ended (8). His vision of the smiting of the temple points to a worldwide dispersion of the Jewish people (9:1-10).

In the end, however, God promises restoration. God will bless His faithful remnant in the future (9:11-15).

Obadiah

Author: The prophet Obadiah (1:1).

Date: Written between 848 and 841 BC.

Title: The book is named after the author, whose name means "servant of the Lord."

Fast Facts

Obadiah spoke of the coming downfall of Edom, an area directly southeast of the Dead Sea that is rich in mountainous terrain. The Edomites had invaded Judah when Jerusalem was being overrun and destroyed by the Babylonians in 587 BC. Obadiah indicates that the Edomites will thus be destroyed.

Note that the Edomites were descendants of Esau. The biblical record indicates that Esau struggled with his brother Jacob even within their mother's womb (Genesis 25:22). Obadiah indicates that the descendants of these brothers continued to struggle.

Summary Outline

1. Edom is doomed (1-9). Obadiah begins this short book by emphasizing the absolute certainty of the impending overthrow of Edom. The judgment is to be thorough and complete. Edom's pride will be debased, its wealth plundered, and its people slaughtered.

2. Edom is denounced (10-14). Edom will be judged because its people are perpetually characterized by aggressiveness, violence, and self-inflated pride.

3. Edom is destroyed (15-21). Edom will thus be shown the same harsh treatment it had shown to Judah (15-16). Whereas Edom will suffer a dark and terrible judgment, Judah will be delivered and will enjoy a bright and beautiful future (17-18). Judah will again possess the land (19-20), and God will rule over His kingdom (21).

Jonah

Author: Jonah, the son of Amittai. Some have argued that perhaps Jonah was not the author because he is referred to in the third person (for example, 1:3,5,9,12). However, Old Testament prophets commonly spoke of their activities in the third person (see for example, Isaiah 37:21; 38:1; 39:3-5; Daniel 1:8).

Date: Written about 760 BC.

Title: The book is named after the author and principal character in the book.

Fast Facts

God sent Jonah, a prophet of the northern kingdom, to witness to the inhabitants of Nineveh, the capital of Assyria. The Assyrians were threatening to overrun Israel, so Jonah resisted the idea of preaching to them and tried to run from God to get out of this assignment. But God providentially manipulated circumstances to bring Jonah to Nineveh, where the people listened to Jonah's message and promptly repented, thereby averting a terrible judgment.

Summary Outline

1. **Jonah's disobedience (1–2).** God commissions Jonah to proclaim judgment against the Ninevites unless they

repent. Not wanting the Ninevites to repent and turn to God (they had a long track record of cruelty toward God's people), Jonah disobeys and instead takes a ship west toward Tarshish. God providentially caused a great fish to swallow Jonah, and he spends three restless days and nights within the great fish.

Jonah knows that God had sovereignly intervened. He cries out to the Lord from the belly of the fish, giving praise and thanksgiving to God for his deliverance. After the three days, God causes the great fish to vomit Jonah out onto dry land.

2. Jonah's obedience (3–4). God once again commissions Jonah to go to Nineveh and warn the people of impending judgment. The entire city repents. Having witnessed their contrition, God holds back the judgment He had intended for the city. This is in keeping with God's policy stated in Jeremiah 18:7-8: "If at any time I announce that a nation or kingdom is to be uprooted, torn down and destroyed, and if that nation I warned repents of its evil, then I will relent and not inflict on it the disaster I had planned."

Jonah is disappointed that the cruel Assyrians are not destroyed, but rather turn to God. God reminds him that He is gracious and forgiving of all people who repent.

Micah

Author: Micah (1:1).

Date: Written about 700 BC.

Title: The book is titled after the author, whose name means "Who is like the Lord?"

Fast Facts

Micah was a simple farmer whose prophetic message confronted the injustices and exploitation he had witnessed. His primary message was that those who were rightly related to God should fight social injustice and reach out to help the poor and disenchanted. He taught that God hates injustice.

Summary Outline

1. Judgment is coming (1–3). Micah pronounces condemnation against Israel for its idolatry (1:1-7) and against Judah for its idolatry and wickedness (1:8–2:13). Both kingdoms will be overthrown because of their unrelenting sin. Nevertheless, God in His mercy and grace will gather a righteous remnant of His people (2:12-13). Micah also denounces the princes and prophets of these kingdoms for their injustices (3).

2. Blessing will follow judgment (4–5). One day God will come to the rescue of His people. He will reinstitute the kingdom, and God's Ruler, the divine Messiah, will rule over the kingdom (5:2-15). There will be both a first coming (5:2-3) and a second coming (5:4-15) of this Ruler.

3. God's case against Israel and the ultimate triumph of His kingdom (6–7). Micah pleads with Israel to do justice, love kindness, and walk humbly with God (6:8). He also reminds these sinful people of God's pardoning grace

(7:18). He closes with a reminder of God's covenant commitment to love His people (7:20).

Nahum

Author: The prophet Nahum (1:1).

Date: Written about 650 BC.

Title: The book is titled after the author.

Fast Facts

Nahum describes the fall and destruction of Nineveh, the Assyrian capital. About 100 years previously, the Ninevites had repented under the preaching of Jonah. Now Nineveh had returned in full force to idolatry, paganism, and brutality. Nahum thus prophesied that even though the Assyrians might seem invincible, their days were numbered, for judgment was rapidly approaching.

Summary Outline

1. Nineveh's destruction is declared (1). Nahum begins by describing God's character (1:2-6). Understanding God's character helps us better understand why God was bringing judgment against Nineveh. God is graceful to those who repent and wrathful against those who turn their backs on Him (1:7-8). Because God is holy, He must necessarily respond to the manifold sins of the Ninevites (1:9-14). The reality of this judgment brings comfort to the people of Judah because it means the threat of potential Assyrian invasions will soon be at an end (1:15).

2. Nineveh's destruction is described (2). Assyria is to be overthrown, and Judah is to be restored (2:1-2). The siege and destruction of Nineveh is described in graphic terms (2:3-13). The Ninevites hardly know what hits them. Nineveh meets a fiery end and is obliterated.

3. Nineveh's destruction is warranted (3). God will destroy Nineveh because the city is brimming with sin, cruelty, rebellion, dishonesty, and corruption (3:1-7). Just as the powerful Assyrians had previously crushed other countries, so now God will crush Nineveh.

═══════ Habakkuk ═══════

Author: The prophet Habakkuk (1:1; 3:1).

Date: Written about 606 BC.

Title: The book is titled after the author.

Fast Facts

Habakkuk was a contemporary of Jeremiah in the seventh century BC. He wrestled with the question of why innocent people suffer while evil people so often seem to prosper. God replied that His people must trust Him, for the wicked will be judged in the end.

Summary Outline

1. Habakkuk's questions and God's answers (1–2).

Habakkuk has two dialogues with the Lord. In the first (1:1-11), the prophet points to the wickedness of Judah and asks God how long He will be silent about it. God answers that He will use the mighty Babylonians as His whipping rod against the people of Judah. The judgment will be swift and violent.

This revelation from God leads to a second dialogue (2). Habakkuk asks why a righteous and holy God will use an evil nation like the Babylonians to bring judgment upon Judah. God answers that He is fully aware of the transgressions of the Babylonians. However, Judah also stands guilty. Therefore, just as the Babylonians stand under condemnation, so does Judah.

2. Habakkuk's hymn of praise to God (3). An enlightened Habakkuk ends his book with a psalm of praise to God (3:1-5). He celebrates the power of God (3:6-12) in recognition of the purpose of God (3:13-19). Habakkuk came to see that God's plan is always best. He gained confidence in God's sovereign purposes, so he expresses joy before the Lord (3:18).

Zephaniah

Author: The prophet Zephaniah, the great-great-grandson of King Hezekiah.

Date: Written about 625 BC.

Title: The book is titled after the author.

Fast Facts

The day of the Lord was approaching, and the fire of God's judgment would have a purifying effect on the nation, melting away their sinful complacency. Yet blessing would eventually come in the person of the Messiah.

Summary Outline

1. Judgment in the day of the Lord (1:1–3:8). Zephaniah predicts God's impending judgment on the entire world because of sin (1:2-3), but he focuses his attention on God's judgment of Judah (1:4-18). Judah's religious leaders were promoting the worship of false pagan deities, and the government officials were engulfed in dishonesty and corruption. The judgment of the day of the Lord was therefore imminent.

Zephaniah predicts massive desolation, unrelenting distress, and terror at every side. Yet, he says, there is still time for repentance, which will turn back God's hand of judgment (2).

Next, Zephaniah pronounces judgment against Philistia, Moab, Ammon, Ethiopia, and Assyria—nations that surrounded Israel. But then he zeroes in on Jerusalem, ripe for judgment in view of its spiritual and moral decadency (3:1-8).

2. God's blessings in the day of the Lord (3:9-20). God's wrathful hand will ultimately bring about a cleansing of the nations (3:8-10). Israel's restoration will follow, with its inhabitants calling on the name of the Lord (3:11-13). The righteous remnant of Israel will be regathered and restored. This will bring joy and jubilation to Israel (3:14-20).

Haggai

Author: The prophet Haggai (1:3).

Date: Written around 520 BC.

Title: The book is named for its author.

Fast Facts

Haggai's words were addressed to the people in Judah and Jerusalem who had returned from exile. He sought to shake them out of their despondency and rejuvenate their spiritual commitment. He urged them to dispel their apathy, set their priorities straight, and rebuild the temple. Blessing would follow.

Summary Outline

1. **A call to rebuild the temple (1).** Haggai reprimands the people for procrastinating in building the temple (1:2-6). They had built their own houses but were indifferent about God's house. Haggai exhorts them to begin rebuilding immediately (1:7-8). He says God had not blessed them because they had forgotten Him (1:9-11). They promptly resumed building the temple (1:12-15).

2. **Future glory for the temple (2:1-9).** When the older generation of Israelites—those who remembered Solomon's glorious temple—saw this smaller, humbler temple,

they were perplexed. It seemed unworthy. Haggai responds with a promise from the Lord that the glory of this temple will be greater than that of the former (2:4-5,9).

3. Future blessing for the people (2:10-19). Haggai reminds the people that evil is contagious (2:10-13) and that they had become contaminated and corrupted by it (2:14-17). However, restoring God to first place in their lives will bring blessing (2:18-19).

4. A messianic prophecy concerning Zerubbabel (2:20-23). To instill a hope in the people, Haggai informs them that one day in the future, the heavens will be shaken (2:20-21), evil people will be overthrown (2:22), and the Messiah will be exalted (2:23). Zerubbabel, a leader among the people, is portrayed as a symbol of the coming Messiah.

*We owe to Scripture the same reverence
which we owe to God.*
JOHN CALVIN (1509–1564)
FRENCH REFORMER

Zechariah

Author: The prophet Zechariah.

Date: Written between 520 and 518 BC.

Title: The book is named for the author, whose name means "the Lord remembers."

Fast Facts

Zechariah was among the first exiles to return to Jerusalem following the exile. He sought to motivate the Jews to cease their apathy and finish rebuilding the temple. Instead of rebuking the people, Zechariah demonstrated the importance of the temple. It was the religious center of Jewish life and represented the presence of the one true God among the Israelites in the midst of a watching pagan world.

Summary Outline

1. Zechariah's night visions (1–6). Zechariah speaks to God's people through a series of eight visions, some communicating comfort and others speaking of judgment:

- God will one day restore and bless His people (1:1-17).
- The nations that have aligned against Israel will be judged (1:18-21).
- God will protect Jerusalem (2).
- Israel will be restored and redeemed by the coming Messiah (3).
- The Holy Spirit will renew the light of Israel (4).
- Individual sin will be judged (5:1-4).
- National sin will be removed (5:5-11).
- God's judgment will fall upon the nations (6).

2. Zechariah's burden (7–8). Zechariah next provides four messages representing his burden for the returned remnant:

- The people's ritual worship had not been focused on God (7:4-7).
- Divine retribution follows disobedience (7:8-14).
- God will gather, restore, and bless Israel (8:1-17).
- There will be much joy among God's people (8:18-23).

3. Oracles concerning the future (9–14). Zechariah closes with two oracles related to the future Messiah: First, the Messiah will be rejected in His first coming, being betrayed for a mere 30 pieces of silver (11:13). Second, just before the Messiah's second coming, Jerusalem will be under attack, and the Jews within the city will cry out to the Messiah for deliverance (12). Israel will then be redeemed (13), and the King (Jesus the Messiah) will come to Jerusalem (the Mount of Olives), after which He will judge the nations and reign over the earth (14).

Malachi

Author: The prophet Malachi.

Date: Written between 433 and 400 BC.

Title: The book is titled after the author, whose name means "the Lord's messenger."

Fast Facts

Malachi prophesied after the temple was rebuilt (515 BC). The people's return to their homeland from exile had not translated into a desire to walk closely with God. They practiced empty rituals. Spiritual lethargy was at an all-time high. God assured them through Malachi that His love for them is unending. Malachi also urged repentance, for more judgment would come if sin continued.

Summary Outline

1. **A reminder of God's love (1:1-5).** The Israelites were so encumbered by difficulties that they were blind to God's love for them. God therefore reminds the people of His special covenant love for them.

2. **God's case against Israel (1:6–3:15).** Despite God's love, the people remained unfaithful to God, engaging in constant sin. The priests showed no respect for God, using diseased animals for sacrifices. The people were indifferent toward God's covenant. The men of the nation were divorcing their wives so they could marry foreign women (2:10-16). Adding insult to injury, the people robbed God by ceasing to bring tithes to Him. Malachi explains that if the people will only repent, God will shower blessings on them (3:7-12). In their arrogance, however, the people remain in sin (3:13-15).

3. **God promises judgment and rewards (3:16–4:6).** Malachi prophesies that in a future day of judgment, God will remember the righteous remnant, sparing them just as a father spares his son (3:16-18). At the coming of the Messiah, the wicked will be condemned (4:1). Their judgment will bring consolation to the righteous (4:2).

Malachi closes the book with a command for the people

to remain obedient to God's law. His prophecies connect the Old and New Testaments, for he predicts that a forerunner will prepare the way for the coming Messiah (4:5-6). This was fulfilled in the ministry of John the Baptist (Matthew 3:1; 11:13-14).

The New Testament

Introduction to the New Testament

The New Testament is a collection of 27 books and epistles composed over a 50-year period by a number of different authors. The primary personality of the New Testament is Jesus Christ. The primary theme is salvation in Jesus Christ, based on the new covenant.

The word *testament* carries the idea of covenant, or agreement. The Old Testament focuses on the old covenant between God and the Israelites. It was a covenant of law. The new covenant focuses on grace and is the basis for the forgiveness of sins in Jesus Christ (Luke 22:20; 1 Corinthians 11:25; Hebrews 7).

The first four books of the New Testament are the Gospels: Matthew, Mark, Luke, and John. Each one contains an account of the life of Christ. None of them portrays all the details of His life, but when we consider them together, we can reconstruct a fairly full account.

Following the Gospels is the book of Acts. This book focuses on how Christianity spread following the death and resurrection of Christ.

Following Acts are the epistles. The apostle Paul wrote 13 of these, and the rest were written by other followers of Jesus. Paul's epistles typically responded to particular issues that specific churches needed help on. Even so, these epistles are relevant to us today because many of the problems that existed in the early church are still issues that we struggle with today. The other (non-Pauline) epistles are more general.

The final book of the New Testament is the book of Revelation, which is an apocalyptic book full of prophecy. This book was written for the purpose of giving its readers hope, inspiration, and comfort in the face of severe persecution. The book demonstrates that in the end God wins, and we will one day live face-to-face with Him forever in a new heaven and a new earth.

Matthew

Author: Matthew (also known as Levi).

Date: Written between AD 50 and 60.

Title: The book is titled after its author, one of the 12 apostles.

Fast Facts

Matthew, a Jew, wrote this Gospel to convince Jewish readers that Jesus is the promised Messiah. It contains about 130 Old Testament citations or allusions (such as 2:17-18; 4:13-15; 13:35; 21:4-5; 27:9-10). Nonetheless, Matthew does not confine the good news to his own people, the Jews, but rather emphasizes that the gospel is for all people.

Summary Outline

1. **The presentation of the King (1:1–4:11).** Matthew's genealogy proves that Jesus is a fulfillment of the Abrahamic and Davidic covenants (1:1-17). John the Baptist prepared the way for Him (3:1-12), and the Father gave verbal approval of Him (3:13-17).

2. **The sermon of the King (4:12–7:29).** Jesus formally began His ministry (4) and then preached the Sermon on the Mount. He addressed the blessed life (5:1-16), the Law (5:17–7:6), prayer (7:7-11), the Golden Rule (7:12), living righteously (7:13-14), true versus false teaching (7:15-20), entering into the kingdom (7:21-23), and the importance of His words (7:24-29).

3. **The miracles of the King (8:1–9:34).** Jesus proved His identity by performing numerous miracles, including healing a leper (8:1-4), a centurion's servant (8:5-13), and Peter's mother-in-law (8:14-17). He also calmed the sea (8:23-27), forgave and healed a paralytic (9:1-8), healed a ruler's daughter (9:18-26), healed two blind men (9:27-31), and delivered a man who was mute and demon-possessed (9:32-34).

4. **Representatives of the King (9:35–11:1).** Jesus chose and trained 12 apostles, who were to spread the good news about the kingdom of heaven. Jesus endowed them with healing power and warned them about the kind of reception they would likely receive.

5. The King is rejected (11:2–16:12). After John the Baptist was rejected (11:2-15), Jesus was also rejected in many cities He visited (11:16-30). The harshest rejection came from the Pharisees (12). In consequence, Jesus delayed His kingdom program until the second coming. He then spoke parables to illustrate what the interim period would be like (13:1-53). Jesus then experienced even further rejection (13:54–16:12).

6. Subsequent teachings of the King (16:13–20:28). Jesus prepared His disciples by teaching them things they'd need to know following His death. He taught them about the church (16:18-20), total commitment (16:24-26), the second coming (16:27-28), faith (17:14-21), humility (18:1-5), evangelism (18:11-14), offense (18:15-20), forgiveness (18:21-35), rich people (19:16-26), how the last will be first (20:1-16), and the danger of ambition (20:20-28).

7. The King enters Jerusalem (20:29–23:39). Jesus then entered Jerusalem as people shouted "hosanna" (21:1-11). He cleansed the temple (21:12-17), condemned fruitless living (21:18-22), and noted how Israel's religious leaders had gone astray (21:28-41; 22–23).

8. Predictions of the King (24–25). Jesus delivered His Olivet Discourse (on the Mount of Olives), in which He prophesied the soon destruction of Jerusalem and its temple. He also prophesied the future tribulation period and His eventual second coming.

9. The passion of the King (26–27). The Jewish leaders plotted to kill Jesus (26:1-5), and Judas betrayed Him (26:14-16). Jesus celebrated the Passover with His disciples

(26:17-25) and instituted the Lord's Supper (26:26-29). At Gethsemane, Jesus prepared for the end while His disciples were supposed to pray (26:36-46). After He was arrested (26:47-56), He was falsely accused (26:57-68), denied by Peter (26:69-75), delivered before Pilate (27:1-2), tried (27:15-25), scourged (27:26-28), and led to Golgotha (27:29-33), where He was crucified (27:34-44) and died (27:45-50).

10. The resurrection of the King (28). Gloriously, three days later, Jesus was resurrected from the dead. The tomb was empty (28:1-8), and Jesus appeared to the women who came there (28:9-10). He also appeared to the disciples (28:16-17). Before ascending to heaven, Jesus gave His disciples the Great Commission (28:18-20).

Mark

Author: Mark, a close companion of the apostle Peter. He accompanied the apostle Paul and Barnabas on part of their first missionary tour (Acts 12:25; 13:5). Near the end of Paul's life, he requested Mark's help (2 Timothy 4:11).

Date: Written around AD 55.

Title: The book is titled after its author.

Fast Facts

Mark's Gospel is the shortest of the four Gospels and was probably written first. It is the most fast-paced and action-packed of the four. About one-third of Mark's Gospel focuses on the last week of Jesus' life on earth, concluding with His death and resurrection. Mark targeted Gentile readers, carefully explaining Jewish customs—something he would not have done if he were targeting Jewish readers.

Summary Outline

1. **Jesus' early Galilean ministry (1:1–3:6).** Mark's Gospel begins with John the Baptist preparing the way for Jesus (1:1-8), after which Jesus was baptized (1:9-11) and tempted by the devil (1:12-13). Jesus began His ministry in and around Galilee, called His disciples (1:16-20), ministered in Capernaum (1:21-34) and Galilee (1:35-45), and defended His ministry against challenges from the scribes and Pharisees (2:1–3:6).

2. **Jesus' later Galilean ministry (3:7–6:13).** Jesus commissioned 12 disciples to be with Him and to preach and drive out demons (3:7-19). He taught parables to reveal the spiritual nature of the kingdom (4:1-25) and demonstrated His authority and power by performing many miracles (4:35–5:43). He then returned to His hometown, where He confronted unbelief (6:1-6) and sent out His disciples to heal the sick and call people to repentance (6:7-13).

3. **Jesus' withdrawal from Galilee (6:14–8:30).** After John the Baptist was beheaded (6:14-29), Jesus withdrew to a quiet place to get away from the crowds (6:30-32). They followed Him, grew to a large size, and He

miraculously fed 5000 men (in addition to women and children) with five loaves and two fish (6:33-44). He walked on water (6:45-52), healed many (6:53-56), continued to rebuke the Pharisees (7:1-23), and performed even more miracles (7:25–8:30).

4. Jesus' journey to Jerusalem (8:31–10:52). Jesus explained that He had to go to Jerusalem, where He would be put to death. Peter tried to stop Him, and Jesus detected Satan behind Peter's words (8:31-38). Jesus revealed His glory to the disciples on the mount of transfiguration (9:1-13). He then rebuked His disciples for their unbelief (9:14-20) and again spoke of His impending death and resurrection (9:30-32).

Jesus instructed the disciples on many matters, including humility (9:33-37), hell (9:42-50), marriage (10:1-12), having childlike faith (10:13-16), the danger of riches (10:17-22), and the difficulty of entering God's kingdom (10:23-31). He spoke again about His death and resurrection (10:32-34) and urged His followers to remain humble (10:35-45). En route to Jerusalem, Jesus healed a blind man (10:46-52).

5. Jesus' Jerusalem ministry (11–13). In fulfillment of messianic prophecy, Jesus rode into Jerusalem on a donkey to cheers of "hosanna" (11:1-11). Nevertheless, the Jewish nation was resolute in its rejection of Jesus (11:12-24). Jesus then cleansed the temple, after which the chief priests questioned His authority (11:27-33). Jesus prophesied the coming destruction of Jerusalem with its temple, as well as His second coming in glory in the end times (13:1-37).

6. Jesus' death and resurrection (14–16). Jesus celebrated the Passover meal with His disciples and instituted the Lord's Supper (14:1-26). He revealed that Peter would deny Him (14:27-31). Meanwhile, the Jewish leaders plotted how to kill Him. A short time later, Jesus prayed in agony in Gethsemane as He awaited the end (14:32-42). He was arrested (14:43-52), tried (14:53-65), taken before Pilate (15:1-15), crucified (15:16-41), and buried in a tomb (15:42-47). Meanwhile, Peter repented of his denial (14:66-72).

Gloriously, as predicted, Jesus was resurrected from the dead three days later and made many appearances to His followers. He proved beyond all doubt that He was alive forevermore (16).

Luke

Author: Luke, a frequent companion of the apostle Paul.

Date: Written in AD 60.

Title: The book is titled after its author.

Fast Facts

Luke was a well-educated and cultured man. He was careful to emphasize that he wrote his Gospel based on reliable, firsthand sources (Luke 1:1-4). Luke, a medical doctor, expressed unflinching belief in Jesus' virgin birth (Luke 1:35) and miracles (see 4:38-40; 5:15-26; 6:17-19; 7:11-15).

Summary Outline

1. Jesus' birth and childhood (1–2). Luke's Gospel begins with an account of the ancestry, birth, and early years of Jesus. It also includes information on John the Baptist, Christ's forerunner.

Even though Jesus is fully God, Luke's Gospel emphasizes that He was also fully man in the Incarnation. He grew in wisdom as a human child, something that could never be said of His divine nature (2:39-40,52).

2. Jesus' preparation for ministry (3:1–4:13). John the Baptist, Christ's forerunner, prepared the way for Christ's coming and ministry (3:1-20). Jesus was baptized by John the Baptist, at which point the Holy Spirit descended upon Him and the Father gave a verbal affirmation of Him (3:21-22). The genealogy Luke provides traces Jesus back to the first man, Adam, showing Jesus' full identification with humanity (3:23-38). Jesus was victorious against the devil's temptations (4:1-13).

3. Jesus' Galilean ministry (4:14–9:50). Jesus formally began His ministry, demonstrating His authority over demonic spirits, diseases of every kind, the realm of nature, the effects of sin, and human tradition (4–6). This demonstration of authority was a necessary prelude to His ministry of preaching and discipling that would subsequently take place (7:1–9:50).

4. The rejection of Jesus (9:51–18:30). As Jesus taught from city to city, He experienced rejection by many, including the Samaritans (9:51-56), a lawyer (10:25-37), Jewish leaders (11:14-36), Pharisees (11:37-44), and more lawyers (11:45-54). The Jewish religious leaders even accused Him of being demonized, after which Jesus pronounced a series of divine woes upon them.

> *Ignorance of the Scripture is ignorance of Christ.*
> JEROME (374–420)
> APOLOGIST

Knowing He would soon be going to Jerusalem, where He would ultimately meet death at the cross, Jesus instructed His disciples on a number of important matters. He addressed hypocrisy (12:1-12), covetousness (12:13-34), faithfulness (12:35-48), repentance (13:1-9), the kingdom (13:18-35; 17:20-37; 18:15-30), relating to people (14), God's love (15), wealth (16), forgiveness (17:1-6), service (17:7-10), gratitude (17:11-19), and prayer (18:1-14).

5. Jesus' arrival at Jerusalem (18:31–19:44). Jesus foretold His death and resurrection to the 12 disciples (18:31-34). Even in the face of impending suffering, however, Christ looked beyond Himself to bring healing to a man (18:35-43) and salvation to a sinner (19:1-10). Jesus spoke a parable indicating that the kingdom of God would not appear immediately and that His followers would need to faithfully carry out the work given to them in His absence. He said He would one day return with authority to judge every man (19:11-27). Jesus then triumphantly entered into Jerusalem (19:28-44).

6. Jesus' death and resurrection (19:45–24:53). After entering Jerusalem, Jesus encountered further opposition from Jewish leaders (19:45–20:47). He spoke to His disciples about the signs of His second coming (21:8-19,25-38) and prophesied the destruction of Jerusalem (21:20-24). He celebrated the Passover with His disciples (22:7-18), during which He predicted His betrayal by Judas (22:21-23) and denial by Peter (22:31-34).

As the end approached, Christ prayed in Gethsemane (22:39-46). He was then betrayed by Judas (22:47-53), denied by Peter (22:54-62), beaten (22:63-65), tried by the Sanhedrin (22:66-71), tried by Pilate (23:1-7), tried by Herod (23:8-12), tried by Pilate yet again (23:13-25), crucified on a cross (23:26-49), and buried (23:50-56).

Gloriously, however, Jesus was resurrected from the dead (24:1-12). He made many appearances to His followers, thereby proving His resurrection (24:13-43). Before ascending into heaven, Christ gave His followers the Great Commission (24:44-53).

===== **John** =====

Author: The apostle John, a close companion of Jesus (13:23; 19:26-27).

Date: Written between AD 85 and 90.

Title: The book is titled after its author.

Fast Facts

John's purpose was to proclaim Jesus as the Savior and Redeemer of the world by presenting convincing proofs of His identity as God, man, and Messiah. The Gospel is evangelistic, persuading people to trust in Christ for salvation (John 20:31). The word *believe* occurs almost 100 times in this Gospel (more than in any other Gospel). John points to many titles of Jesus, including these:

- Lord (6:23; 11:2; 20:20; 21:12)

- Son of God (1:49; 5:25; 10:33; 11:4,27)

- Son of Man (3:14-15; 5:27; 6:27,62; 9:35)

- Teacher or Rabbi (1:38,49; 3:2; 4:31; 6:25; 9:2; 11:8; 20:16)

- King (1:49; 12:13; 18:33,37)

- Messiah or Christ (1:41; 4:25-26; 11:27)

John demonstrated that Jesus has the attributes of deity, including omniscience (4:29), omnipresence (14:23), and preexistence (1:1; 8:58; 17:5). The miracles He performed further attest to His divine identity (for example, John 2:23; 5:1-15). John also demonstrated that in the Incarnation, Jesus was fully human (John 1:14).

Summary Outline

1. **Jesus' Incarnation (1:1-18).** In the prologue of John's Gospel, we find two pivotal points that lay a foundation for the rest of the book: Jesus is absolute deity and has eternally dwelt with the heavenly Father (1:1), and Jesus became a human being in order to reveal the Father to humanity (1:18).

2. **Jesus' public ministry (1:19–12:50).** In this section of John's Gospel, we find Jesus under careful scrutiny by

Israel. He performed seven signs (miracles) to prove His identity as the promised Messiah. Jesus turned water into wine (2:1-11), healed a nobleman's son (4:46-54), healed a paralytic (5:1-16), miraculously fed a vast multitude of people (6:1-13), walked on water (6:16-21), gave sight to a blind man (9:1-7), and raised Lazarus from the dead (11:1-44).

As Jesus performed these miracles, or signs, some believed in and received Him. Many others rejected Him. In fact, as the signs unfold throughout the Gospel, the opposition to Christ intensifies.

3. Jesus' private ministry to His disciples (13–17). In view of the increased opposition to Him, Christ prepared His disciples by teaching them what they would need to know following His death, which was less than 24 hours away. He encouraged them not to worry, but to trust in Him (14:1-4). He urged them to remain obedient and pray in His name (14:8-15). He promised that they would be indwelt by the Holy Spirit, who would empower them (14:16-21; 16:1-15). He instructed them to abide in Him as a branch abides in a vine (15:1-11).

Jesus then predicted His death and resurrection (16:16-33). He prayed for Himself (17:1-5), for His disciples (17:6-19), and for all believers (17:20-26).

4. Jesus' crucifixion and resurrection (18–21). The Gospel closes with a dramatic description of Christ's arrest and His trials before Annas, Caiaphas, and Pilate (18:1–19:16). Jesus died on the cross as the Lamb of God who takes away the sin of the world (19:17-37; see also

1:29). Gloriously, though, Jesus rose from the dead three days later. He made multiple appearances to His followers, proving beyond any possible doubt that He had risen (20–21).

Acts

Author: Luke, a close companion of the apostle Paul. (The book of Acts may be considered part 2 of Luke's Gospel.)

Date: Written in AD 61, about a year after Luke wrote his Gospel.

Title: Some Bible versions title this the Acts of the Apostles. In reality, the book predominantly focuses on the continuing acts of Jesus through the apostles by the power of the Holy Spirit.

Fast Facts

Whereas Luke's Gospel contains an orderly account of the accomplishments of Jesus during His earthly life, the book of Acts contains an orderly account of the accomplishments of Jesus, through the church and by the power of the Holy Spirit, in the 30 years following His resurrection and ascension. Acts serves as a link between the four Gospels and the epistles. The book chronicles how Christianity miraculously spread among both Jews and Gentiles around the northern Mediterranean, including Samaria (Acts 8:5-25); Phoenicia, Cyprus, and Antioch

(9:32–12:25); Phrygia and Galatia (13:1–15:35); Macedonia (15:36–21:16); and Rome (21:17–22:29).

Acts is a book of transitions: from Judaism to Christianity, from law to grace, and from Jews alone as the people of God to Jews *and* Gentiles as the people of God.

Summary Outline

1. **The Christian witness to Jerusalem (1:1–8:3).** Acts picks up where the Gospels left off. In the Gospel accounts, Jesus appears to His followers to prove His resurrection. In the book of Acts, Jesus continues to appear to His followers for 40 days (1:3).

The risen Lord instructed His followers to stay in Jerusalem so the promise concerning the Holy Spirit would be fulfilled. It occurred a week and a half later, and the disciples became supernaturally empowered by the Holy Spirit.

Filled with new courage, the disciples boldly proclaimed the message of the resurrected Lord. Peter's sermon, focusing largely on Jesus' resurrection, led to 3000 conversions (2). Thousands of other conversions occurred as a result of further messages and healings from the apostles (3:1–5:16).

The explosive growth of Christianity was not without problems in the early church. The apostles were persecuted and imprisoned because of their witness (5:17-42). Not all the needs were being met within the church, and for this reason deacons were appointed (6:1-8). Stephen, a faithful witness, was brought before the Sanhedrin and ordered to be executed (6:9–7:60).

2. The Christian witness to Judea and Samaria (8–12). The good news of the gospel was preached to the Samaritans—people hated by the Jews—and many became believers. By apostolic authority, the Holy Spirit was imparted to these new members of the body of Christ just as the Spirit had earlier been imparted to Jewish believers in Christ on the day of Pentecost (8:5-40). All are one in Christ.

God soon after brought Saul to faith in Christ, and he became an apostle to the Gentiles (9:1-31). Meanwhile, the Lord taught Peter that the barrier between Jews and Gentiles had been brought down, and the Gentiles were thus welcome to God's salvation (9:32–11:18).

The persecution against the church progressively increased. But the church also continued to explosively grow throughout the Roman Empire.

3. The Christian witness to the ends of the earth (13–28). Paul went on three missionary tours (13–14; 15:36–18:22; 18:23–21:16), spreading God's Word in strategic cities like Antioch, Perga, Iconium, Lystra, Derbe, Troas, Philippi, Thessalonica, Berea, Athens, Corinth, Ephesus, Galatia, and Miletus. Paul's strategy was to visit major Roman capitals that were easily reached by existing trade routes, a strategy that resulted in the gospel spreading out to other areas.

By God's providence, Paul was often thrown in jail, and from there he wrote many of his epistles to different churches (Ephesians, Colossians, Philippians, and so forth).

Romans

Author: The apostle Paul (1:1).

Date: Written about AD 57.

Title: Paul was writing to the Christians at the church in Rome (1:7,11-15).

Fast Facts

Rome was a hub city connected by road to numerous other cities in the ancient world. It was thus a strategic city in the spread of the gospel. The church at Rome was predominantly made up of Gentile believers (1:5,13; 11:13; 15:15-16). However, there was also a strong minority of Jewish believers (2:17; 9–11; 14). The apostle Paul had a strong desire to visit the church of Rome (1:10-15). Apparently, he wrote this letter to prepare the way for his eventual visit to the city (15:14-24).

Romans is the most theological of all of Paul's letters. Paul spoke of humanity's sin problem and the universal need for righteousness (1:18–3:20); salvation and how one is declared not guilty before God by placing faith in Christ (3:21–5:21); how a believer experientially grows in righteousness in daily life, how he is freed from the power of sin, and how he is freed from the domination of the law (6–8); how the Jews have a special place in God's plan (9–11); instructions on life in the body of Christ (12); the need for respecting the government (13:1-7); and unity between Jews and Gentiles (15:5-13).

Summary Outline

1. **The theme (1:1-17).** The apostle Paul expresses his desire to minister in Rome. He also states the theme of the book—the gospel of salvation.

2. **The need for righteousness (1:18–3:20).** All people stand condemned. The Gentiles stand condemned because they have suppressed the knowledge of God they have gained from "general revelation"—that is, from God's revelation in the world of nature and their inner conscience (1:18-32). The Jews also stand condemned by God because they have failed to live up to God's infinitely righteous standards. Paul, himself a Jew, provides a reality check for his fellow Jews by reminding them that they have consistently failed to obey God's law (2:17-29) and have failed to believe God's Word (3:1-8). Everyone stands guilty before God.

3. **The imputation of righteousness (3:21–5:21).** On their own, people cannot possibly attain the righteousness that leads to salvation. God's solution is to impute righteousness to those who believe in Christ. This is the doctrine of justification. Justification involves not only acquitting believing sinners of all sin but also imputing the very righteousness of Christ to their account. This justification is not something that can be earned, but rather is entirely by God's grace (3:21-24), based on the blood sacrifice of Jesus (3:25-26). It is a gift that is received by faith alone (3:27-31).

This principle of justification apart from works is illustrated in the life of Abraham (4). And the wonderful thing about justification is that it brings reconciliation between God and man (5:1-11). The first Adam brought condemnation, but the last Adam, Jesus Christ, brings imputation of righteousness (5:12-21).

4. **The imparation of righteousness (6–8).** Paul speaks about not only the *imputation* of righteousness but also the *impartation* of righteousness. More specifically, Paul reveals that the believer is positionally dead to the principle of sin (6:1-14) as well as the practice of sin (6:15-23). Union with Jesus Christ makes the sanctified life possible. Because of what Christ has accomplished, the Christian has been set free from the law (7). As well, the Holy Spirit indwells and empowers every believer, making the sanctified life possible now (8:1-17). Better yet, one day Christians will be entirely set free from the presence of sin when they are glorified in heaven (8:18-39).

5. **The vindication of righteousness (9–11).** Paul turns his attention to the salvation of the Jews, God's chosen people. He speaks of the past spiritual privileges of Israel (9), Israel's present state of unbelief (10), and Israel's future prospect of restoration (11). Israel as a nation was set aside because of unbelief, yet Israel has a future and will be grafted back into the promised blessing according to God's covenant promises. Righteousness will thereby be vindicated.

6. **The application of righteousness (12–16).** Romans closes with an exhortation for believers to live out their salvation. This exhortation comes last in the book because behavior is built upon belief. Paul mentions the Christian's

duty to God (12), to the state in which he lives (13), and to other people (14–16).

> *Leave not off reading the Bible till you*
> *find your hearts warmed...Let it not only*
> *inform you, but inflame you.*
> THOMAS WATSON (1620–1686)
> PURITAN PREACHER

===== **1 Corinthians** =====

Author: The apostle Paul.

Date: Written in AD 55.

Title: This was the first letter Paul wrote to "the church of God in Corinth" (1:2).

Fast Facts

Corinth was a strategic center in Greece, the hub of commerce from the north to the south and from the east to the west. The population was a mix of Roman, Egyptian, Greek, and Asian. A gospel message proclaimed in Corinth was likely to find its way to the distant regions of the inhabited earth.

Corinth's moral character also made it a fertile field for the gospel. The city contained the temple of Aphrodite, the Greek goddess of love, with 1000 priestesses (prostitutes). This led to sexual debauchery all over the city. The Greek word *korinthiazomai*, meaning literally "to act the Corinthian," came to mean "to practice fornication."

Paul had done missionary work in Corinth. After he moved on to Ephesus, he received notice that there were problems in Corinth. He wrote this epistle to address these problems.

Summary Outline

1. Introduction (1:1-9). Paul opens with a greeting of grace and a prayer of thanksgiving.

2. Disunity in the church (1:10–4:21). Paul addresses divisions within the church—some favoring Paul, others favoring Apollos, and others favoring Peter (1). Such factions are not spiritual (2), but rather are immature (3). We must center ourselves in Christ, not in human leaders (4).

3. Immorality in the church (5–6). A case of incest festered within the church, and the church had taken no disciplinary action. Paul orders the church to remove the offender from fellowship until he repents (5).

Paul urges church members to stop taking legal action against each other. He encourages them to settle differences within the Christian community (6).

4. Marriage (7). Paul answers the Corinthians' questions about marriage, celibacy, divorce, and remarriage.

5. Food offered to idols (8–10). Next, Paul addresses the balance between Christian liberty and the law of love. Specifically, should a Christian eat food that has been offered to an idol? Corinthian Christians disagreed on the issue. Paul indicates it is sometimes best to limit liberty to avoid the possibility of offending a weaker brother over a minor matter.

6. Worship in the church (11–14). Paul addresses several issues related to public worship, including improper observance of the Lord's Supper and the improper use of spiritual gifts.

7. The resurrection (15). Pagan cultists in Corinth denied the idea of a resurrected body, so Paul includes substantive instruction on Christ's resurrection, its importance to Christianity, and the nature of the resurrection body.

8. Personal closing (16). Paul ends his letter by providing instructions for a collection he intended to make for poor believers in Jerusalem (16:1-4). He closes with a few exhortations and greetings (16:5-24).

═══ 2 Corinthians ═══

Author: The apostle Paul.

Date: Written in AD 56.

Title: This was the second letter Paul wrote "to the church of God in Corinth" (1:1).

Fast Facts

Paul in this letter defends his God-given authority as an apostle of God. False prophets had penetrated the Corinthian church and assaulted Paul's character and authority. Some of the Corinthians had apparently believed their lies and rebelled against Paul. These false teachers were leading the people astray, and unless Paul acted decisively, the entire church might have become engulfed in false doctrine.

Paul had intervened and made a "painful visit" to them (2:1). He followed up this visit with a severe letter, which is no longer in our possession (2:4). Later, Titus passed on news to Paul that the majority of Corinthian believers had repented of their rebellion against him (7:7). Grieved at past strained relations, Paul wrote this letter to the Corinthians to clarify his ministry and his calling and authority as an apostle. He also sought to bring unity to the church.

Summary Outline

1. **Introduction (1:1-11).** Paul opens with thanksgiving to God.

2. **Paul's change of plans (1:12–2:13).** Paul explains why his visit to Corinth had been delayed. It was not for any lack of desire. Rather, he wants them to have plenty of time to repent (1:12–2:4). (False teachers had turned some of the people against Paul.) Paul also requests that they graciously restore a repentant man to fellowship who had formerly been especially antagonistic toward him (2:5-13).

3. **The nature of Christian ministry (2:14–6:10).** Paul offers the Corinthians a defense of his ministry, his message, his circumstances, his motives, and his conduct. He does this because some in the church had called some of this into question.

4. **Exhortations to the Corinthians (6:11–7:16).** Paul exhorts the Corinthian believers to keep themselves separate from all that could bring defilement (6:11–7:1). He informs them of the great comfort he took at the news of their change of heart toward him (7:2-16).

5. Paul's collection for the saints (8–9). The Macedonian Christians had been very liberal in their giving to the needy brethren in Jerusalem (8:1-6). Paul desired that the Corinthian believers do the same (8:7–9:15). He lets them know that God will reward their generosity.

6. Paul vindicates his apostleship (10–13). Paul offers a defense of his apostolic authority and his credentials. This is apparently aimed at a small minority of church members who remained in rebellion against him (10). In establishing his credentials as an apostle, Paul mentions his knowledge, personal integrity, visions from the Lord, miraculous acts, and more (11:1–12:13).

Paul reveals his desire to visit the Corinthians again and urges full repentance of all church members so that he will not have to speak severely when he comes (12:14–13:10). He closes the letter with exhortations, personal greetings, and a Trinitarian benediction (13:11-14).

Galatians

Author: The apostle Paul.

Date: Written in AD 50.

Title: Paul wrote this letter "to the churches in Galatia" (1:2).

Fast Facts

Apparently, Judaizers infiltrated some of Paul's congregations and challenged his credentials. Paul confirms his authority as a genuine apostle of Jesus Christ (Galatians 1:10–2:21).

These Judaizers accused Paul of removing Jewish legal requirements (such as circumcision) in order to make the gospel more appealing to Gentiles. Their purpose was therefore to "Judaize" these Gentile believers—to persuade them that after believing in Christ, they must take an additional step and be circumcised, eat only the right kinds of foods, and participate in certain Jewish feast days (see Acts 15:24; 20:29-30).

> The Bible is alive, it speaks to me; it has feet,
> it runs after me; it has hands, it lays hold on me.
> MARTIN LUTHER (1483–1546)
> REFORMER

This effectively added works to grace, and Paul would not have it (4:20). Salvation is a gift that is received by faith in Christ (3:6-9). Paul even says that if anyone delivers to the church any other gospel than the one previously handed down (including a gospel from Judaizers), they are under God's curse (1:8). Salvation is by grace alone, Paul says, and Gentiles need not become Jews in order to be true Christians.

Summary Outline

1. Introduction (1:1-10). Paul begins by affirming he is an apostle by divine appointment (1:1-5). He expresses dismay at the Galatians' departure from grace (1:6-10).

2. Paul defends his apostleship (1:11–2:21). Paul's gospel of justification, in which the believing sinner is made right with God by grace through faith, came not from men but from God (1:11-24). This message of justification was backed by the other apostles in Jerusalem (2:1-10). However, Paul had to publicly correct Peter on the issue of law versus grace (2:11-21).

3. Paul defends the true gospel (3–4). Paul argues that the Galatians began their spiritual journey by faith, and now they must continue in faith (3:1-5). Just as Abraham was justified by faith, so all believers are justified by faith (3:6-9). Believers have been redeemed from the curse of the law (3:10-18). Besides, the law was never intended to save people, but rather to drive them to faith (3:19-22). Believers are no longer bound by the law (3:23–4:7). Indeed, the law conflicts with the freedom we have in Christ (4:8-31).

4. The call to godliness (5–6). The greatest enemy to Christian liberty is legalism (5:1-12). But believers must also be cautious not to fall into lawlessness (5:13–6:10). Christians are set free not only from bondage to the law but also bondage to sin.

Ephesians

Author: The apostle Paul.

Date: Written in AD 61.

Title: Paul wrote this letter "to God's holy people in Ephesus" (1:1).

Fast Facts

Ephesus was a city characterized by luxurious homes, elegant buildings, and wide avenues. It was a leading commercial and trade center of the ancient world and one of the more prominent cities in the province of Asia.

The city was well-known for its temple of the Roman goddess Diana, a structure that was considered one of the seven wonders of the world. Consequently, this city was brimming with pagans.

During the apostle Paul's third missionary tour, he spent about three years in Ephesus, building up the church there (Acts 19). When he left, his young associate Timothy pastored there for another year or so, seeking to establish the believers in sound doctrine (1 Timothy 1:3,20). Paul wrote his epistle to the Ephesians while a prisoner in Rome in AD 61.

Summary Outline

1. **The position of Christians (1–3).** Chapters 1–3 contain no commands, but chapters 4–6 contain more than 30. Paul provides the doctrinal basis for living in chapters 1–3 and then draws the practical application of that doctrine in chapters 4–6.

Paul first addresses issues related to the Christian's heavenly position, including adoption, redemption, inheritance, power, life, grace, citizenship, and Christ's love. Paul also notes that the triune God is intimately involved in our salvation—the Father chose us (1:3-6), Jesus attained our redemption at the cross (1:7-12), and the Holy Spirit sealed us (1:13-14). Through this salvation, Jews and Gentiles become one in the body of Christ (2:11-23; 3:6).

2. The practice of Christians (4:1–6:9). In view of the wondrous doctrines provided in chapters 1–3, Paul urges believers to live lives that are worthy of their high calling (4:1). Paul demonstrates how doctrine affects duty. Because we are positionally *in* Christ, we are now to walk *for* Christ as we live on earth. Toward this end, we must walk in unity (4:1-16), in holiness (4:17-32), in love (5:1-6), in the light (5:7-14), and in wisdom (5:15–6:9).

3. The protection of Christians (6:10-24). Paul closes by exhorting believers to put on the whole armor of God to stand against the powers of darkness (6:10-20). Christians are especially to utilize the sword of the Spirit, which is the Word of God.

Philippians

Author: The apostle Paul.

Date: Written in AD 63.

Title: Paul wrote this letter "to all God's holy people in Christ Jesus at Philippi" (1:1).

Fast Facts

Philippi was a Roman colony. Apparently, the Jewish population was too small to establish a synagogue, which required a minimum of ten adult Jewish men (women were not allowed to act as substitutes). The Jews therefore

met for prayer by the river Gangitis on the Sabbath, and
that is where Paul addressed the first converts of Philippi
during his second missionary tour.

After a time, the Philippian church developed some
problems. It came to suffer under intense rivalries (2:3-4),
disturbances caused by Judaizers (3:1-3), and libertinism
(3:18-19). These internal problems severely hindered spiritual growth, so Paul wrote this letter to help the Philippian
church overcome them.

Summary Outline

1. **Paul's present circumstances (1).** Paul begins by
expressing thanks for the Philippians' continued support
of his ministry (1:1-11). Paul was presently in prison, but
he nevertheless rejoiced because of the continued spread
of the gospel (1:12-26). Paul was eager to depart this life
and be with Christ in heaven (1:21-23). But he also recog-
nized the need for him to remain on earth to continue his
work of ministry (1:27-30).

2. **Humility in the Christian life (2).** Because of the
disunity and rivalry in the church, Paul urged the Philippians to pursue humility, which goes a long way toward
bringing unity (2:1-4). Christ Himself is our greatest
example of humility (2:5-11). Such humility leads to self-
sacrificial living (2:12-30).

3. **Knowing Christ (3).** The apostle Paul, before his
conversion to Christ, was firmly committed to a life of
legalism. Indeed, he was a Hebrew of Hebrews. Paul now
said, however, that such legalistic pursuits were as nothing

compared to the goal of knowing Christ. He emphasized that true righteousness is not gained through external obedience to the law (such as the Judaizers taught), but is received through faith in Christ.

4. Experiencing the peace of Christ (4). Again addressing the problem of disunity, Paul urged the Philippians to live in unity with each other, to pursue holiness, and to prayerfully depend on God. As we cast our anxious requests on Him, we experience the indescribable peace of God. Paul boasts that he can do all things through the power of Christ—a power that is also available to his Philippian brethren (4:10-20).

Colossians

Author: The apostle Paul.

Date: Written in AD 61.

Title: Paul wrote this letter "to God's holy people at Colossae" (1:2).

Fast Facts

Colossae was about 100 miles east of Ephesus. Paul had never been to the city, but he had heard about the church there from his associate Epaphras (1:7-8). Some of the news he heard, however, bothered him, so he wrote this epistle to the Colossian believers while he was in prison.

Summary Outline

1. **The supremacy of Jesus Christ (1–2).** One of the

Colossians' key problems was their tendency to mix Christianity with other philosophies and religions. The church contained both Greeks and Jews, and some of them—especially the Jews—evidently incorporated some of their former religious ideas into Christianity. By holding onto Jewish food laws and festivals (2:16), circumcision (2:11), mysticism (2:18), and an inflated view of angels (2:18), these Jewish Christians had brought some un-Christian elements into the church.

Paul answered such ideas by urging the Colossians not to let anyone judge them concerning food laws or the need to observe holy days or festivals (2:16). He said believers have a spiritual circumcision in Christ and do not need a physical circumcision (2:11). He warned against the "idle notions" that can result from mysticism (2:18). He argued for the supremacy of Christ over all things (1:15), including the world of angels. Christ Himself created the angels, so He alone is to be worshipped, not the angels (1:16; 2:18).

2. Submission to Jesus Christ (3–4). The foundation for the spiritual life is not Jewish philosophy or legalism, but rather the believer's union with Christ (3:1-4). Because of the believer's union with Christ and His death, the believer must regard himself as dead to sin and therefore put sin aside (3:5-11). Because of the believer's union with Christ and His resurrection, the believer must count himself as alive unto righteousness (3:12-17). This righteousness ought to show itself in relationships between husbands and wives, parents and children, masters and slaves, and Christians and outsiders (3:18–4:6).

1 Thessalonians

Author: The apostle Paul.

Date: Early AD 51.

Title: This is Paul's first letter "to the church of the Thessalonians" (1:1).

Fast Facts

Thessalonica was a capital of the Roman province of Macedonia in northern Greece. It was a prosperous port. Paul founded the church of Thessalonica around AD 50 during his brief visit there. He would have stayed longer, but the Jews resisted Paul when some of their own number converted to Christianity. For Paul's safety, the Christians in Thessalonica sent him to Berea (Acts 17:1-10).

Summary Outline

1. **Paul's personal commendation to the Thessalonians (1–3).** Paul expressed heartfelt thanks for the Thessalonian Christians' spiritual transformation, including their firm eternal hope, full of faith and love (1). Paul also answered some false charges of troublemakers who had attacked his character and his message. He did this by reminding the Christians in Thessalonica about what he had actually accomplished among them. He reminded them that he had even refused financial support so no one could impugn his motives (2). Meanwhile, Paul had sent Timothy to minister among them and was now comforted

to hear Timothy's report that the Thessalonians had grown in their faith and love (2:17–3:10).

2. Paul's practical exhortation to the Thessalonians (4–5). Paul now answers several of the Thessalonians' questions. He explains that in contrast to the pagans, they ought to seek sexual purity (4:1-8). He also urges that there should be no idlers in the church, complacently waiting for the coming of the Lord. Everyone should work with his own hands instead of sponging on the generosity of fellow Christians (4:9-12).

The Thessalonians were concerned about believers who had died and how this might relate to the future rapture of the church. Paul informs them that the dead in Christ will rise first, and then the living will be transformed into their resurrection bodies to meet them in the air (4:13-18).

Paul also provides instructions on the eschatological day of the Lord (5:1-11). He closes with a few instructions on holy living (5:12-22).

2 Thessalonians

Author: The apostle Paul.

Date: Written in AD 51.

Title: This is the second letter Paul wrote "to the church of the Thessalonians" (1:1).

Fast Facts

Paul probably wrote 2 Thessalonians from Corinth

during the summer of AD 51, several months after he wrote 1 Thessalonians. He now wrote 2 Thessalonians to further explain and clarify God's program of events relating to the day of the Lord (including Christ's second coming). He also encouraged the believers to correct the disorders remaining among them.

> *Bible study is like eating peanuts.*
> *The more you eat, the more you want to eat.*
> PAUL LITTLE (1928–1975)
> EVANGELIST, INTERVARSITY CHRISTIAN FELLOWSHIP

Summary Outline

1. **Comforting words in the midst of persecution (1).** Paul begins with thanks to God for the Thessalonians' faith and love as well as their firm stand for Christ in the face of persecution (1:1-4). He assures them that those who are causing them suffering will one day be irrevocably punished at the second coming of Christ (1:5-12).

2. **The day of the Lord (2).** Some phony epistles had surfaced teaching that the day of the Lord had already come, and some of the Thessalonian brethren were apparently concerned. Paul responds that certain noticeable events will take place before this eschatological day comes, including the emergence of the antichrist and various social upheavals (2:1-12).

3. **Exhortations to prayer and discipline (3).** Paul closes by exhorting the Thessalonians to pray on his behalf as they continue to wait patiently for the second coming (3:1-5):

Paul also deals with the proper attitude they should have as they await Jesus' return. On the one hand, believers should be constantly ready for Christ's coming. On the other hand, people who are so caught up in prophetic excitement that they stop working and live off others are to be rebuked (3:6-13). Balance is necessary.

1 Timothy

Author: The apostle Paul.

Date: Written between AD 62 and 64.

Title: This was Paul's first letter to Timothy, his "true son in the faith" (1:2).

Fast Facts

Timothy was Paul's young and trusted colleague. He converted to Christianity during Paul's visit to Lystra and grew quickly in his spiritual life. Paul trusted Timothy so much that Timothy became a leader in the church and even represented Paul to various churches (Acts 17:14-15; 1 Corinthians 4:17).

Paul writes as a mature, experienced pastor to a young, inexperienced pastor.

Summary Outline

1. **Paul's instructions on doctrine (1).** Paul warns young Timothy about the danger of false doctrine (1:3-11). He urges Timothy to defend biblical doctrine at all costs. He

also urges Timothy to fulfill his calling in ministry with no compromises (1:12-20).

2. Paul's instructions on worship (2–3). Paul instructs Timothy on the roles of men (2:1-8) and women (2:9-15) in the church. He then offers qualifications for elders (3:1-7) and deacons (3:8-13).

3. Paul's instructions on false teachers (4). Paul advises Timothy on some issues that came up with some false teachers, such as marriage, food, and exercise. Paul urges Timothy to watch his doctrine closely.

4. Paul's instructions on people in the church (5). Paul advises the younger pastor how to treat people in the church (5:1-2), focusing specifically on widows (5:3-16) and elders (5:17-20). Paul's underlying idea is that Timothy ought to treat other people as he would his own family.

5. Paul's instructions on the man of God (6). Paul closes with a warning about the unbiblical idea that godliness results in material blessing. The pastor ought to focus on godliness and be content with what he has (6:3-16). The man of God ought to crave godliness and not money.

2 Timothy

Author: The apostle Paul.

Date: Written between AD 66 and 67.

Title: This is the second letter Paul wrote to Timothy, his "dear son" (1:2).

Fast Facts

Paul wrote 2 Timothy from prison and expected to be executed shortly (4:6). This letter contains Paul's last words to Timothy. Paul encouraged Timothy to maintain the faith, hold on to sound doctrine, be faithful in ministry, and preach the gospel relentlessly (1:6,13-14; 3:15–4:5).

Summary Outline

1. **The perseverance of a man of God** (1). Paul encourages Timothy to stand firm in the power of the gospel and not give way to fear, intimidation, or shame. Persecution will come, but God sustains His servants.

2. **Characteristics of a faithful minister** (2). Paul encourages Timothy to disciple and teach others (2:1-2), be single-minded in serving the Lord (2:3-5), patiently endure all things (2:6-13), work diligently for the Lord (2:14-19), pursue righteousness and avoid youthful lusts (2:20-23), and be gentle as a servant of God (2:24-26).

3. **The coming apostasy** (3). Paul warns Timothy of an impending time of apostasy. People will increasingly fall prey to empty religiosity and false teaching (3:1-9). Arrogance, godlessness, deception, and persecution will increase. Timothy must therefore stand strong in his defense of the Word of God (3:10-17). Paul reminds Timothy that all Scripture is inspired by God and sufficient to equip people for the work of ministry.

4. **Preach the Word** (4:1-5). Paul exhorts Timothy to be ready to preach the Word in season and out of season.

Many will abandon sound doctrine, but Timothy is to do the work of an evangelist and fulfill his ministry.

5. Paul's impending death (4:6-22). Paul reveals that the time of his departure (death) is near. He is content because he has fought the good fight, finished the race, and kept the faith. He expresses one last wish to see Timothy again, but regardless, he has full faith that God will preserve him for the heavenly kingdom.

Scripture is the royal chariot in which Jesus rides.
CHARLES SPURGEON (1834–1892)
PASTOR, LONDON

Titus

Author: The apostle Paul.

Date: Written between AD 62 and 64.

Title: Paul wrote this letter to Titus, whom he calls "my true child in our common faith" (1:4).

Fast Facts

Titus was a young pastor and the leader of the church in Crete. He was one of Paul's trusted inner circle of friends and ministry associates (2 Corinthians 8:23). Titus was an uncircumcised Gentile who illustrated Paul's teaching that Gentiles need not be circumcised to be saved.

Summary Outline

1. Appointing elders (1:1-9). Paul charges Titus, a pastor in Crete, to organize the churches there by appointing elders. These elders were to meet certain spiritual qualifications and help protect against the false teachers Paul warns about in the verses that follow.

2. Rebuking false teachers (1:10-16). Paul focuses heavy attention on warning against false teachers (1:10-16). The nature of the false teaching is not entirely clear, though it seems to relate to "Jewish myths," circumcision, genealogies, and Jewish legalism (1:10,14; 3:9-10). The flock (church) must be protected and the false teachers silenced (1:11).

3. Sound doctrine and good works (2–3). Paul thus urges Titus and his congregations to pursue sound doctrine and good works (1:9; 2:1–3:11). History reveals that the people who lived in Crete were belligerent, argumentative, uncontrolled, and resentful of authority. Consequently, Paul insists not only that Titus teach with authority but also that the teaching of the Word of God leads to good works. For example, believers must show respect to civil government (3:1-7), respect each other (3:8-15), and avoid disputes and divisions.

Philemon

Author: The apostle Paul.

Date: Written about AD 63.

Title: Paul wrote this short letter to Philemon, whom he calls "our dear friend and fellow worker" (1:1).

Fast Facts

Philemon was Paul's friend and a leader of the church at Colossae. He was a prominent man who had owned a slave named Onesimus, who escaped, became a believer, and was now returning under Paul's counsel.

Summary Outline

1. A prayer of thanksgiving (1-7). Paul begins by offering a prayer of thanksgiving for Philemon's Christian faith and love.

2. Paul's petition for Onesimus (8-16). Onesimus, a slave, had escaped from Philemon's household and probably went to Rome. Perhaps Onesimus reasoned that in the booming population of Rome, no one would notice him. He ended up meeting the apostle Paul in prison (we are not told how this meeting actually came about). Under Paul's leading, Onesimus became a Christian.

Paul developed a sincere love for young Onesimus. Paul was fully aware that under Roman law, Onesimus could be executed as a runaway slave. But amends had to be made. Paul sent Onesimus back to Philemon with a letter urging Philemon to set Onesimus free as a brother in Christ so that he could return to help Paul in his work of ministry. Paul urges Philemon to forgive Onesimus just as Christ had forgiven Philemon.

3. Paul's promise to Philemon (17-25). Paul closes by placing any debt Onesimus might have to his own account. He trusts that Philemon would do the right thing before the Lord.

Hebrews

Author: Unknown. The most likely possibilities include the apostle Paul, Apollos, and Barnabas.

Date: Written about AD 68.

Title: The earliest manuscripts have the simple title "To the Hebrews."

Fast Facts

Hebrews describes itself as a brief "word of exhortation" (13:22). It draws heavily on the Old Testament and urges Hebrew Christians to remain steadfast in their commitment to Christ and His cause. These Jewish believers were going through a severe period of persecution (see 10:32-34).

For a Jew to become a believer in Christ in the first century required sacrifice. Such a believer was immediately branded as an apostate and a blemish to the Jewish nation. He was considered unclean and expelled from the synagogue, his children could not attend school at the synagogue, and he lost his job. Furthermore, the Jewish high priest could throw him into jail (10:33-34). At first, these Jewish Christians joyfully accepted persecution. But after a while, it became too much for them to bear, and their endurance weakened (10:35-36).

They never entertained thoughts of renouncing Jesus Christ, but they considered drifting back into the outward observances of Judaism—including rituals, ceremonies, and sacrifices (6:1-2). They apparently reasoned that if they externally took part in such Jewish rituals, the Jewish leaders might be satisfied and leave them alone.

This "word of exhortation" teaches that Jesus is the ultimate fulfillment of the Old Testament and is greater than all Old Testament institutions (1:5–7:28). To step back into Judaism in whatever form is unacceptable. The author of Hebrews calls his readers to move on to maturity in the Christian faith (6:1).

Summary Outline

1. **Christ is superior (1:1–4:13).** In making the case to these Jewish believers not to regress back into the external practices of Judaism, but instead to move on to Christian maturity, the author lays out convincing evidences that Christ is superior to the Old Testament prophets (1:1-3), superior to the entire angelic realm (considered by Jews to be the mediators of the Mosaic law) (1:4–2:18), and superior to Moses (3:1–4:13). Obviously, to move away from Christ and back toward Judaism would be folly.

2. **Christ's work is superior (4:14–10:18).** Christ is superior not only in His person but also in His work. Indeed, Christ has a superior priesthood (4:14–7:28), He brought about a superior covenant (8), and He offered Himself as a superior sacrifice (9:1–10:18).

3. **The assurance and endurance of faith (10:19–13:25).** The author therefore urges his Jewish readers to persevere in holding fast to their Christian confession of faith (10:19–11:40), for there is great danger in falling away (10:26-39). The author defines the nature of faith (11:1-3)

and provides many examples of faith (11:4-40). These examples of faith ought to be an encouragement to these discouraged Jewish Christians. The writer urges his readers to endure in their faith and not give up (12:1-29).

James

Author: James (1:1).

Date: Written between AD 44 and 49.

Title: The book is named after its author.

Fast Facts

James was the oldest half-brother of Jesus and leader of the Jerusalem church (Acts 12:17). He was also one of the pillars of the early church (Galatians 2:9).

James wrote to Jewish Christians ("to the twelve tribes"—1:1) who were in danger of giving only lip service to Jesus. This situation may have arisen as a result of the persecution of Herod Agrippa I (Acts 12). Perhaps some of these Jewish Christians had become a little gun-shy about living the Christian life. James's intent, therefore, is to distinguish true faith from false faith. He shows that true faith results in outward works—visible evidences of faith's invisible presence.

The lifestyle James expects of the true believer includes control of the tongue (3), submission to God (4), a right attitude toward money (5:1-6), and patience in the midst of suffering (5:7-12).

Summary Outline

1. **Trials and temptations (1:1-18).** Everyone has trials and temptations. These constitute tests of our faith (1:2-12). James argues that God allows us to encounter these trials because they mature our faith and increase our patient endurance as we depend upon God.

2. **Evidences of a living faith (1:19–5:6).** James stresses the importance of righteous conduct that grows out of a living faith. It is not enough to be a hearer of God's Word; one must be a doer of God's Word (1:22-25). He stresses that faith without works is dead (2:14-27), meaning that believers' faith in Christ must show itself in the way they live. Those who merely claim to have faith but do not show that faith in the way they live have a spurious faith.

True faith not only empowers Christians to obey the Word of God (1:19-27) but also shows itself in the way they treat other people. For example, people of faith do not discriminate against others (2:1-13). Nor do they misuse their tongues with others (3:1-12). People of true faith grow in wisdom (3:13-18), they are humble in their interactions, they avoid lust and licentious living (4:1-12), and they openly depend on and submit to God (4:13–5:6).

3. **The triumph of faith (5:7-20).** James closes this letter by encouraging his readers to patiently endure their sufferings in view of the future prospect of the coming of the Lord (5:7-12). Regardless of the trials that inevitably surface in life, believers can rest assured that God has a purpose for allowing His children to encounter them. A

strong prayer life is vitally important, for the prayers of righteous people are powerful and can even bring healing and restoration to believers who fall into sin (5:13-20).

1 Peter

Author: The apostle Peter.

Date: Written in AD 63 or 64.

Title: This is the first letter Peter wrote.

Fast Facts

Peter was a fisherman who became one of the 12 men who were with Jesus throughout His earthly ministry. Peter was also one of the "inner three" who saw some of Jesus' greatest miracles and saw Him in His true glory (Mark 9; 2 Peter 1:16-18).

This letter was sent to scattered groups of Christians in the five Roman provinces that covered the greater part of modern Turkey. Peter probably wrote from Rome at the outbreak of Nero's persecution. Having already endured beating at Herod's hands, Peter wrote his brethren in Asia probably to encourage and strengthen them in facing the Neronian persecution. He may well have recalled his Lord's injunctions: "Strengthen your brothers" (Luke 22:32) and "Feed my sheep" (John 21:15-17).

Peter was crucified upside down in Rome during Nero's persecution in AD 64.

Summary Outline

1. The believer's salvation (1:1–2:12). Christians enjoy a living hope through the resurrection of Christ from the dead. A wondrous inheritance awaits all believers in heaven (1:1-4). This future hope gives strength to Christians as they suffer trials in the present (1:5-9). The proper response of the Christian to this salvation ought to be a life of holiness (1:13–2:12).

2. The believer's submission (2:13–3:12). Submissiveness is Christlike. Christians give a good testimony of their commitment to the Lord by their submission to the government (2:13-17), to masters (2:18-25), within marriage (3:1-8), and even in the face of evil or bad circumstances (3:9-12).

3. The believer's suffering (3:13–5:14). Recognizing that his readers will experience increasing opposition to Christianity, Peter exhorts them to be ready to defend their faith and conduct (3:13-16). If they must suffer at all, Peter writes, it ought to be for the sake of righteousness and not because of sin (3:17).

Peter then instructs his readers in how they should live. They are not to pursue the lusts of the flesh, but rather the will of God (4:1-6). They ought to show mutual love toward one another (4:7-11). If they are slandered for their faith, they should not be shaken, but rather recognize that God will bring judgment to persecutors in the end (4:12-19). Meanwhile, church elders must keep watch over their flocks (5:1-4). All should pursue humility (5:5-7), pray, resist the devil, and stay strong in the faith, trusting the God of all grace (5:8-14).

2 Peter

Author: The apostle Peter.

Date: Written in AD 66.

Title: This is the second letter Peter wrote.

Fast Facts

Peter wrote this letter to the same groups he addressed in his first letter. The apostle's goal was to correct some errors that had penetrated certain churches—specifically, that morality was unimportant and that Jesus Christ would not return. Apparently, some mystics were placing more weight on their own spiritual experiences than on the prophets' and apostles' revelations that Jesus would one day return. Peter rebuked these ideas and emphasized that Jesus will in fact return and that people should live their lives in accordance with that belief.

Summary Outline

1. **Growing in Christian character (1).** Peter desires that his readers come to a true knowledge of Jesus Christ (1:1-2). This includes the recognition that believers are recipients of great and precious promises (1:3-4). In view of such blessings, believers ought to divorce themselves from the corruption of the world and pursue Christian virtues instead (1:5-7). Doctrinal beliefs must give way to virtuous practice (1:8-11).

Peter knew his death was near. He accordingly urges

his readers to hold fast to the truth and never forget the riches of their position in Christ (1:12-21). He knew what he was talking about, for he was an eyewitness of Christ's glory (1:16-18), and he knew that Scripture was inspired by God (1:21).

2. Warnings about false prophets and teachers (2). Knowing that his time is short, Peter writes against false teachers who emerged from within the church and endangered the flock (2:1-3). These false teachers rejected authority, sought self-gratification, denied the Lord by the way they lived, and exploited others for profit. Peter thus warns his followers about them and affirms that a dire punishment from God awaits these false teachers (2:4-22).

3. Christ will return (3). Peter closes by speaking about the certainty of Christ's return. Many people will scoff at the idea (3:1-7). However, God's Word assures us that it will happen. If God is delaying the second coming, He is showing mercy, for He desires that there be plenty of time for people to be saved (3:8-10). The reality of Christ's coming is a strong incentive to Christian living and spiritual maturity (3:11-18).

1 John

Author: The apostle John.

Date: Written in about AD 90.

Title: This is the first letter John wrote.

Fast Facts

By the time the aging apostle John wrote this letter, Christianity had already been around for more than 50 years. Plenty of time had passed for spiritual and doctrinal errors to develop. The primary heretical system John battles seems to be an early strain of Gnosticism. Apparently, some Gnostic teachers were conducting itinerant ministries in John's congregations and seeking converts. John wrote this letter to warn true followers of Christ against such heresies.

A prime idea in Gnosticism is that spirit is good but matter is evil. If this is true, then Christ could not have become human, because a human body (matter) would be evil. This position thus argued that a spiritual Christ entered into the body of a human Jesus at His baptism and left the body of the human Jesus before the crucifixion. This scenario avoids the idea that Christ Himself became material and died on the cross.

Summary Outline

1. **Conditions for fellowship (1:1–2:27).** John had regularly fellowshipped with Christ, so he desired to share with his readers how they may share that same fellowship with Christ (1:1-4). To enjoy this fellowship, however, they must meet certain conditions, including walking in the light (1:5-7). By *light*, John seems to be pointing to God's truth, pure living, and repentance of all known sin. People cannot live in darkness (that is, live in unrepentant sin) and claim to fellowship with God. But those who walk in the light enjoy fellowship with God.

Of course, Christians still have the sin nature, and therefore we are not perfect. Whenever we commit sin, we must confess that sin to God so that fellowship may thereby be restored (1:8-10). If we fall into sin, Jesus Christ, our Advocate, pleads our case with the Father (2:1-2). Satan may accuse us, but Jesus is our defense attorney.

To know God is to be obedient to Him. We cannot claim to know God if we remain in disobedience (2:3-6). We must also love Christian brothers and sisters. We cannot claim to be walking in the light while at the same time hating our brothers or sisters (2:7-14).

John warns against loving the things of the world. Such things hinder fellowship with God (2:15-16). Moreover, we must not hold to false doctrines about Jesus Christ. More specifically, we must not hold to the Gnostic idea that Jesus (the man) and Christ (the spirit) are two distinct entities. Rather, we must believe the truth that Jesus *is* the Christ. In the Incarnation, eternal God truly took on a human nature (2:18-27).

2. Characteristics of fellowship (2:28–5:3). If we are truly fellowshipping with God, that fellowship will show itself in certain characteristics. For example, we will seek to habitually manifest purity in our lives (2:28–3:3). We will pursue righteousness (3:4-12) and will seek to love in both deed and in truth (not mere lip service) (3:13-24). We will seek to love as Christ loved (4:7-21). Love for God is irrevocably connected with keeping God's commandments (5:1-3).

3. Consequences of fellowship (5:4-21). Our fellowship

with God leads to victory over the world (5:4-5), assurance of salvation (5:6-13), confidence in prayer (5:14-17), and freedom from habitual sin (5:18-21). Again, this does not imply we become morally perfect, but rather that Christ gives us the power and freedom not to habitually sin.

2 John

Author: The apostle John.

Date: Written about AD 90.

Title: This is the second letter John wrote.

Fast Facts

Second John is one of the shortest epistles in the New Testament. It deals with the same problem as 1 John—Gnostic errors that were threatening the church.

Summary Outline

1. Walk in truth and love (1-6). John teaches that his readers should walk in truth and love. The question is this: To whom was John writing? There are two possible viewpoints—the literal view and the personification view.

The literal view affirms that John was writing to a literal family. John opens by writing, "The elder, to the lady chosen by God and to her children" (1). The word *chosen* may point to the prominence of this woman. John later mentions the lady's sister, who is chosen by God (13) and who may have been another prominent woman.

The other view is that John personified a particular church as a chosen lady and her members as children. The fact that the church is elsewhere referred to as the bride of Christ shows that using feminine terms to speak of the church is appropriate (2 Corinthians 11:2; Ephesians 5:22-33; Revelation 19:7). John says that he and "all who know the truth" love this lady (1), which may fit better with a local church than a particular woman. Moreover, the exhortation in verse 5 that we should love one another seems strangely inappropriate when directed to a woman and her children, but it would be perfectly fitting in a church context. The closing—"the children of your sister, who is chosen by God, send their greetings" (13)—sounds as if the members of one church are sending greetings to another church.

Perhaps John wrote this way to protect church members in the event that the epistle ended up in the hands of Roman persecutors. If the letter were discovered, the Romans would think this epistle was a private letter to a friend, and the church would remain safe.

2. Avoid false teachers (7-13). John was dealing with an early strain of Gnosticism. His main concern was the Gnostic denial of the humanity of Christ. The root of the problem was the Greek idea that the spiritual and material (physical) realms are entirely separate and have nothing to do with each other. In this line of thinking, spirit is good but matter is evil. Some false teachers, therefore, argued that the spiritual Christ could not have actually had a material, human body.

The Gnostics denied Christ's humanity in one of two

ways. Some, called Docetists, claimed that Jesus had only the appearance of flesh without substance or reality (like a phantom). (*Docetism* comes from a Greek word, *dokeo*, meaning "to seem" or "to appear.") Jesus' suffering and death on the cross, they said, was not real, for the body was not real.

Other Gnostics, following the lead of Cerinthus, believed the spiritual Christ entered into a human (physical) Jesus at the time of his baptism (in the form of a dove) and left the human Jesus before the crucifixion. History reveals that Cerinthus lived in Ephesus toward the end of the first century, which was also where the aged apostle John lived.

John's goal in this letter was to commend truth and to warn against deceivers who taught heresy concerning Christ—specifically, the heresy of denying that Christ came in the flesh (7). John said that those who teach such things should not be received (10).

3 John

Author: The apostle John.

Date: Written about AD 90.

Title: This is the third letter John wrote.

Fast Facts

Third John is one of the shortest books in the Bible. It is one of the five or six New Testament letters addressed to a single individual. Whereas 2 John warns against receiving heretics, 3 John condemns the lack of hospitality shown to faithful ministers of the Word.

Summary Outline

1. **The commendation of Gaius (1-8).** Gaius was both godly (2-4) and generous (5-8). He is therefore worthy of commendation.

2. **The condemnation of Diotrephes (9-14).** By contrast, Diotrephes was full of pride and ambition. He loved to be preeminent, refused to recognize John's apostolic authority, and refused hospitality to faithful ministers of the Word (9-11).

John closes this brief letter with a recommendation of Demetrius and a benediction (13-14).

Jude

Author: Jude (1:1).

Date: Written between AD 70 and 80.

Title: The book is titled after its author.

Fast Facts

Jude was a younger brother of Jesus and James. Earlier in his life, Jude had rejected Jesus as the divine Messiah (see John 7:1-9). Following Jesus' resurrection from the dead, he and his brothers converted (Acts 1:14). Jude went on to become a church leader in Jerusalem. He refers to himself as "a servant of Jesus Christ" (Jude 1). Jude's short letter is apologetic in the sense that it seeks to defend Christianity against error.

> Read the Scripture, not only as a history,
> but as a love-letter sent to you from God.
>
> THOMAS WATSON (1620–1686)
> PURITAN PREACHER

Summary Outline

1. Jude's purpose (1-4). Jude's goal was to exhort his readers to contend for the faith once for all entrusted to the saints. "The faith" refers to the body of Christian truth handed down by the apostles.

2. False teachers who threaten Christianity (5-16). The particular false teachers Jude refuted were heretics who denied that Jesus was the Son of God and turned Christian liberty into a license to sin. They were teaching that being saved by grace opens the door for Christians to freely sin because these sins will no longer be held against them.

Jude thus urges Christians to hold fast to the truth and to stand against false teachers seeking to infiltrate the church. He affirms that God will punish and destroy false teachers. He also reminds his readers of God's past dealings with those who felt free to sin, including the unbelieving Israelites, the wicked people of Sodom and Gomorrah, and even the wicked angels (5-7). Woe unto those who think they can so easily get away with sin!

3. Defending against false teachers (17-23). The apostles had previously warned that such false teachers would emerge (17-19). Jude thus encourages his readers to guard against the onslaught of apostasy (20-21). As they mature in the Christian faith, they will be able to rescue others from false doctrine (22-23).

4. Doxology (24-25). This glorious doxology points us to the sustaining power of Jesus Christ.

Revelation

Author: The apostle John.

Date: Written around AD 95.

Title: This book contains its own title: "The Revelation from Jesus Christ" (1:1).

Fast Facts

The book of Revelation is the only apocalyptic book in the New Testament.

The apostle John had been exiled on the isle of Patmos in the Aegean Sea for the crime of sharing the good news about Jesus Christ (1:9). It was on this island that John received the revelation.

The recipients of the book were undergoing severe persecution. In fact, some of their number had been killed, and things were about to get even worse. John wrote this book to give his readers a strong hope that would help them patiently endure their suffering.

Summary Outline

Revelation 1:19 provides an outline of the book of Revelation: "Write, therefore, what you have seen, what is now and what will take place later." John recorded the things he had seen in chapter 1, where we find a description of Jesus in His present glory and an introduction to the book of Revelation. "What is now" refers to the present circumstances of the seven churches of Asia Minor recorded in Revelation 2–3. "What will take place later" refers to futuristic prophecy of the tribulation period, second coming, millennial kingdom, and eternal state described in Revelation 4–22.

1. **The things you have seen (1).** A blessing is pronounced on all who read the book of Revelation (1:1-3). John sees Christ in all of His glory (1:9-20; see Daniel 7). The Lord gives John special strength and commands him to write.

2. **The things that are (2–3).** Here we find a description of the seven churches of Asia Minor: Ephesus, Smyrna, Pergamum, Thyatira, Sardis, Philadelphia, and Laodicea. The churches are symbolized in the book of Revelation as lampstands, probably because they are intended to bear God's light in this dark world (compare with Matthew 5:16). As Jesus reveals in Revelation 2–3, however, they do not always succeed and are often in need of correction. Still, Jesus commends those churches that were worthy of commendation. He promises a reward for those who correct their shortcomings.

3. **The things that are to take place later (4–22).** We first read of a heavenly scene, including a description of

the glory of God's throne (4) and the reception of the sealed scroll (5).

Seal judgments. The seal judgments involve bloodshed and war, famine, death, economic upheaval, a deadly earthquake, and cosmic disturbances (6).

Trumpet judgments. The trumpet judgments include hail and fire mixed with blood, the sea turning to blood, water turning bitter, further cosmic disturbances, affliction by demonic scorpions, and the death of a third of humanity (8:6–9:21).

Various unfolding events. A variety of events unfold, including war in heaven (12:7-12), war on earth (12:13-17), the rise of the antichrist and the false prophet (13), the emergence of 144,000 Jewish-Christian evangelists (14:1-5), and the three angels' announcements (14:6-13).

Bowl judgments. The bowl judgments involve horribly painful sores on human beings, more bodies of water turning to blood, the death of all sea creatures, people being scorched by the sun, rivers drying up, total darkness engulfing the land, a devastating earthquake, widespread destruction, and much more (16). During this time, right at the very end of the tribulation period, the final horrific battles of humanity escalate—a campaign of battles known as Armageddon (16:16).

Second coming. At the height of all this, Jesus Christ—the King of kings and Lord of lords—will return to the earth in glory at the end of the tribulation period and set up His kingdom (19:11-16). The second coming will involve a visible, physical coming of the glorified Jesus (see 1 Timothy 6:14;

Titus 2:13; 1 Peter 4:13). It will be a universal experience in the sense that "every eye" will witness the event (Revelation 1:7). Moreover, the second coming will be accompanied by magnificent signs in the heavens (Matthew 24:29-30).

Millennial kingdom. Christ will then set up His millennial kingdom. He will reign on earth for 1000 years in perfect peace, righteousness, and justice (see Revelation 20:2-7; see also Psalm 2:6-9; Isaiah 65:18-23; Jeremiah 31:12-14,31-37; Ezekiel 34:25-29; 37:1-13; 40–48; Daniel 2:35; 7:13-14; Joel 2:21-27; Amos 9:13-14; Micah 4:1-7; Zephaniah 3:9-20).

Eternal state. After the millennium, the wicked dead will be judged at the great white throne judgment and thrown into the lake of fire (20:11-16). Following this, the new heaven and new earth will appear (21:1), the new Jerusalem (the heavenly city) will descend upon the new earth (21:2-8), and Christians will live forever with God in this city (21:9–22:5).

Staying Anchored in God's Word

The word *Bible* means "book." It is appropriate that this bite-size handbook ends with the recognition that the Bible is God's book for *us*. The Bible is much like a manufacturer's handbook that instructs us how to operate our lives.

The Bible is also like an eyeglass. Without the eyeglass, we do not see clearly. We see only a blurred reality. But with the eyeglass, all comes into clear focus. We see God as He really is.

The Bible is also like a lamp. It sheds light on our path and helps us to see our way clearly. Psalm 119:105 says, "Your word is a lamp for my feet, a light on my path."

The Bible is also like food (Hebrews 5:12; 1 Peter 2:2). It gives us spiritual nourishment. If we do not feed on God's Word, we become spiritually malnourished.

The Bible is also like a love letter or Valentine card from God to us (John 3:16-17). It reveals how God's great love for us motivated Him to send Jesus into the world to die for our sins so we could be saved.

Lastly, the Bible is like an anchor. Just as an anchor keeps a boat from floating away, so the Bible is an anchor for us. It prevents us from being swept away when a tidal wave of adversity comes our way.

Let us resolve to daily anchor ourselves on God's Word!

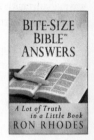
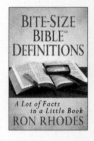